Contents

About mathematics in the National Curriculum

The programmes of study for mathematics

General teaching requirements

The attainment targets for mathematics

Foreword

The National Curriculum lies at the heart of our policies to raise standards. It sets out a clear, full and statutory entitlement to learning for all pupils. It determines the content of what will be taught, and sets attainment targets for learning. It also determines how performance will be assessed and reported. An effective National Curriculum therefore gives teachers, pupils, parents, employers and their wider community a clear and shared understanding of the skills and knowledge that young people will gain at school. It allows schools to meet the individual learning needs of pupils and to develop a distinctive character and ethos rooted in their local communities. And it provides a framework within which all partners in education can support young people on the road to further learning.

Getting the National Curriculum right presents difficult choices and balances. It must be robust enough to define and defend the core of knowledge and cultural experience which is the entitlement of every pupil, and at the same time flexible enough to give teachers the scope to build their teaching around it in ways which will enhance its delivery to their pupils.

The focus of this National Curriculum, together with the wider school curriculum, is therefore to ensure that pupils develop from an early age the essential literacy and numeracy skills they need to learn; to provide them with a guaranteed, full and rounded entitlement to learning; to foster their creativity; and to give teachers discretion to find the best ways to inspire in their pupils a joy and commitment to learning that will last a lifetime.

An entitlement to learning must be an entitlement for all pupils. This National Curriculum includes for the first time a detailed, overarching statement on inclusion which makes clear the principles schools must follow in their teaching right across the curriculum, to ensure that all pupils have the chance to succeed, whatever their individual needs and the potential barriers to their learning may be.

Equality of opportunity is one of a broad set of common values and purposes which underpin the school curriculum and the work of schools. These also include a commitment to valuing ourselves, our families and other relationships, the wider groups to which we belong, the diversity in our society and the environment in which we live. Until now, ours was one of the few national curricula not to have a statement of rationale setting out the fundamental principles underlying the curriculum. The handbooks for primary and secondary teachers include for the first time such a statement.

This is also the first National Curriculum in England to include citizenship, from September 2002, as part of the statutory curriculum for secondary schools. Education in citizenship and democracy will provide coherence in the way in which all pupils are helped to develop a full understanding of their roles and responsibilities as citizens in a modern democracy. It will play an important role, alongside other aspects of the curriculum and school life, in helping pupils to deal with difficult moral and social questions that arise in their lives and in society. The handbooks also provide for the first time a national framework for the teaching of personal, social and health education. Both elements reflect the fact that education is also about helping pupils to develop the knowledge, skills and understanding they need to live confident, healthy, independent lives, as individuals, parents, workers and members of society.

Rt Hon David Blunkett
Secretary of State for Education
and Employment

Sir William Stubbs
Chairman, Qualifications
and Curriculum Authority

About this booklet

This booklet:

- sets out the legal requirements of the National Curriculum in England for mathematics
- provides information to help teachers implement mathematics in their schools.

It has been written for coordinators, subject leaders and those who teach mathematics, and is one of a series of separate booklets for each National Curriculum subject.

The National Curriculum for pupils aged five to 11 is set out in the handbook for primary teachers. The National Curriculum for pupils aged 11 to 16 is set out in the handbook for secondary teachers.

All these publications, and materials that support the teaching, learning and assessment of mathematics, can be found on the National Curriculum web site at www.nc.uk.net.

About mathematics in the National Curriculum

The structure of the National Curriculum

The programmes of study[1] set out what pupils should be taught, and the attainment targets set out the expected standards of pupils' performance. It is for schools to choose how they organise their school curriculum to include the programmes of study for mathematics.

The programmes of study

The programmes of study set out what pupils should be taught in mathematics at key stages 1, 2, 3 and 4 and provide the basis for planning schemes of work. When planning, schools should also consider the general teaching requirements for inclusion, use of language and use of information and communication technology that apply across the programmes of study.

The **Knowledge, skills and understanding** in the programmes of study identify the main aspects of mathematics in which pupils make progress:

At key stage 1	At key stage 2	At key stages 3 and 4
■ number	■ number	■ number and algebra
■ shape, space and measures	■ shape, space and measures	■ shape, space and measures
	■ handling data	■ handling data.

There are requirements for using and applying mathematics in each of these sections.

At key stage 1, teaching should ensure that appropriate connections are made between the sections on number, and shape, space and measures.

At key stage 2, teaching should ensure that appropriate connections are made between the sections on number; shape, space and measures; and handling data.

At key stages 3 and 4, teaching should ensure that appropriate connections are made between the sections on number and algebra; shape, space and measures; and handling data.

These aspects are developed through a range of practical activities using mathematical ideas as set out in **Breadth of study**.

The *Framework for teaching mathematics* provides detailed objectives for planning and teaching mathematics for pupils aged five to 11. Those schools that fully implement the *Framework* will fulfil their statutory duty in relation to the National Curriculum for mathematics at key stages 1 and 2.

[1] The Education Act 1996, section 353b, defines a programme of study as the 'matters, skills and processes' that should be taught to pupils of different abilities and maturities during the key stage.

Schools may find the DfEE/QCA exemplar scheme of work for key stage 3 helpful to show how the programme of study and attainment targets can be translated into practical, manageable teaching plans.

Mathematics at key stage 4

In mathematics there are two programmes of study at key stage 4 – foundation and higher. Pupils may be taught either the foundation or the higher programme of study. The higher programme of study is designed for pupils who have attained a secure level 5 or above at the end of key stage 3.

Attainment targets and level descriptions

The attainment targets for mathematics set out the 'knowledge, skills and understanding that pupils of different abilities and maturities are expected to have by the end of each key stage'[2]. Attainment targets consist of eight level descriptions of increasing difficulty, plus a description for exceptional performance above level 8. Each level description describes the types and range of performance that pupils working at that level should characteristically demonstrate.

In mathematics there are four attainment targets:
- using and applying mathematics
- number and algebra
- shape, space and measures
- handling data.

The level descriptions provide the basis for making judgements about pupils' performance at the end of key stages 1, 2 and 3. At key stage 4, national qualifications are the main means of assessing attainment in mathematics.

Range of levels within which the great majority of pupils are expected to work		Expected attainment for the majority of pupils at the end of the key stage	
Key stage 1	1–3	at age 7	2
Key stage 2	2–5	at age 11	4
Key stage 3	3–7	at age 14	5/6

Assessing attainment at the end of a key stage

In deciding on a pupil's level of attainment at the end of a key stage, teachers should judge which description best fits the pupil's performance. When doing so, each description should be considered alongside descriptions for adjacent levels.

Arrangements for statutory assessment at the end of each key stage are set out in detail in QCA's annual booklets about assessment and reporting arrangements.

[2] As defined by the Education Act 1996, section 353a.

Learning across the National Curriculum

The importance of mathematics to pupils' education is set out on page 14. The handbooks for primary and secondary teachers also set out in general terms how the National Curriculum can promote learning across the curriculum in a number of areas such as spiritual, moral, social and cultural development, key skills and thinking skills. The examples below indicate specific ways in which the teaching of mathematics can contribute to learning across the curriculum.

Promoting pupils' spiritual, moral, social and cultural development through mathematics

For example, mathematics provides opportunities to promote:

- *spiritual development*, through helping pupils obtain an insight into the infinite, and through explaining the underlying mathematical principles behind some of the beautiful natural forms and patterns in the world around us
- *moral development*, helping pupils recognise how logical reasoning can be used to consider the consequences of particular decisions and choices and helping them learn the value of mathematical truth
- *social development*, through helping pupils work together productively on complex mathematical tasks and helping them see that the result is often better than any of them could achieve separately
- *cultural development*, through helping pupils appreciate that mathematical thought contributes to the development of our culture and is becoming increasingly central to our highly technological future, and through recognising that mathematicians from many cultures have contributed to the development of modern day mathematics.

Promoting key skills through mathematics

For example, mathematics provides opportunities for pupils to develop the key skills of:

- *communication*, through learning to express ideas and methods precisely, unambiguously and concisely
- *application of number*, through using and applying the knowledge, skills and understanding of mathematics
- *IT*, through developing logical thinking; using graphic packages and spreadsheets to solve numerical, algebraic and graphical problems; using dynamic geometry packages to manipulate geometrical configurations and using databases and spreadsheets to present and analyse data
- *working with others*, through group activities and discussions of mathematical ideas
- *improving own learning and performance*, through developing logical thinking, powers of concentration, analytical skills and reviewing approaches to solving problems
- *problem solving*, through selecting and using methods and techniques, developing strategic thinking and reflecting on whether the approach taken to a problem was appropriate.

Promoting other aspects of the curriculum

For example, mathematics provides opportunities to promote:

- *thinking skills,* through developing pupils' problem-solving skills and deductive reasoning
- *financial capability,* through applying mathematics to problems set in financial contexts
- *enterprise and entrepreneurial skills,* through developing pupils' abilities to apply mathematics in science and technology, in economics and in risk assessment
- *work-related learning,* through developing pupils' abilities to use and apply mathematics in workplace situations and in solving real-life problems.

The programmes of study for mathematics

A common structure and design for all subjects

The programmes of study

The National Curriculum programmes of study have been given a common structure and a common design.

In each subject, at each key stage, the main column **1** contains the programme of study, which sets out two sorts of requirements:

- **Knowledge, skills and understanding 2** – what has to be taught in the subject during the key stage
- **Breadth of study 3** – the contexts, activities, areas of study and range of experiences through which the **Knowledge, skills and understanding** should be taught.

Schools are not required by law to teach the content in grey type. This includes the examples in the main column [printed inside square brackets], all text in the margins **4** and information and examples in the inclusion statement.

The programmes of study for English, mathematics and science

The programmes of study for English and science contain sections that correspond directly to the attainment targets for each subject. In mathematics this one-to-one correspondence does not hold for all key stages – see the mathematics programme of study for more information. In English, the three sections of the programme of study each contain **Breadth of study** requirements. In mathematics and science there is a single, separate set of **Breadth of study** requirements for each key stage.

The programmes of study in the non-core foundation subjects

In these subjects (except for citizenship) the programme of study simply contains two sets of requirements – **Knowledge, skills and understanding** and **Breadth of study**. The programmes of study for citizenship contain no **Breadth of study** requirements.

Information in the margins

At the start of each key stage, the margin begins with a summary **5** of the main things that pupils will learn during the key stage. The margins also contain four other types of non-statutory information:

- notes giving key information that should be taken into account when teaching the subject
- notes giving definitions of words and phrases in the programmes of study
- suggested opportunities for pupils to use information and communication technology (ICT) as they learn the subject
- some key links with other subjects indicating connections between teaching requirements, and suggesting how a requirement in one subject can build on the requirements in another in the same key stage.

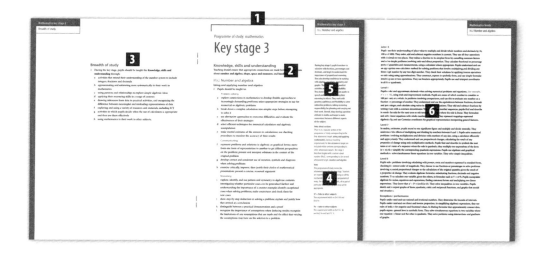

The referencing system

References work as follows:

A reference in ...	... reads ...	... and means ...
Physical education key stage 2	11a, 11b → links to other subjects These requirements build on Gg/2c.	Physical education key stage 2, requirements 11a and 11b build on geography (key stage 2), paragraph 2, requirement c.
Art and design key stage 1	4a → links to other subjects This requirement builds on Ma3/2a, 2c, 2d.	Art and design key stage 1, requirement 4a builds on mathematics (key stage 1), Ma3 Shape, space and measures, paragraph 2, requirements a, c and d.
Citizenship key stage 3	1a → links to other subjects This requirement builds on Hi/10, 13.	Citizenship key stage 3, requirement 1a builds on history (key stage 3) paragraphs 10 and 13.

The attainment targets

The attainment targets **6** are at the end of this booklet. They can be read alongside the programmes of study by folding out the flaps.

The importance of mathematics
Mathematics equips pupils with a uniquely powerful set of tools to understand and change the world. These tools include logical reasoning, problem-solving skills, and the ability to think in abstract ways.
Mathematics is important in everyday life, many forms of employment, science and technology, medicine, the economy, the environment and development, and in public decision-making. Different cultures have contributed to the development and application of mathematics. Today, the subject transcends cultural boundaries and its importance is universally recognised. Mathematics is a creative discipline. It can stimulate moments of pleasure and wonder when a pupil solves a problem for the first time, discovers a more elegant solution to that problem, or suddenly sees hidden connections.

The huge number project

How long would a traffic jam be with 1,000,000 cars in it?

First of all we measured Mr Jones's Ford Orion, it came out at 4.15 metres.

$$4.15$$
$$\times 1,000,000$$
$$\overline{4,150,000}$$

We worked out that 1,000,000 Ford Orions would be 4,150,000 m.

We needed to change that into km. So we divided it by 1,000.

$$4,150,000$$
$$\div 1,000$$
$$\overline{4,150 \text{ km}}$$

Then we hit a problem. We realised that there would be a gap in between the cars of about 1 m.

So that would add on 1,000,000 m

$$5,150,000$$
$$\div 1000$$
$$\overline{5,150 \text{ km}}$$

Then we used an atlas to see what countries the first car would have reached by the time the last one left London.

Maths is the study of patterns abstracted from the world around us – so anything we learn in maths has literally thousands of applications, in arts, sciences, finance, health and leisure!

Professor Ruth Lawrence, University of Michigan

Mathematics is not just a collection of skills, it is a way of thinking. It lies at the core of scientific understanding, and of rational and logical argument.

Dr Colin Sparrow, Lecturer in Mathematics, University of Cambridge

Maths is the truly global language. With it, we convey ideas to each other that words can't handle – and bypass our spoken Tower of Babel.

Professor Alison Wolf, Head of Mathematical Sciences Group, Institute of Education, University of London

If you want to take part in tomorrow's world, you'll need mathematics and statistics just as much as grammar and syntax.

Professor Robert Worcester, Chairman, Market Opinion Research International

Since the age of ten, I've been hooked on mathematical problems as intellectual challenges. However, nobody has to worry that pure mathematics won't be used. Mathematics – even some of the most abstruse mathematics that we thought would never be used – is now used every time you use your credit card, every time you use your computer.

Professor Andrew Wiles, Princeton University

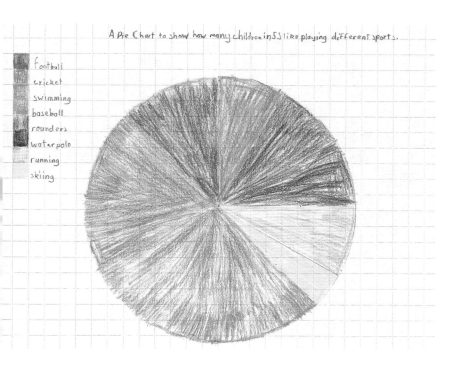

A Pie Chart to show how many children in 5S like playing different sports.

Football
cricket
swimming
baseball
rounders
waterpolo
running
skiing

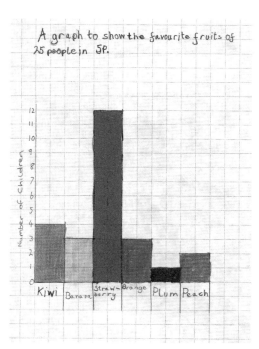

A graph to show the favourite fruits of 25 people in 5P.

During key stage 1 pupils develop their knowledge and understanding of mathematics through practical activity, exploration and discussion. They learn to count, read, write and order numbers to 100 and beyond. They develop a range of mental calculation skills and use these confidently in different settings. They learn about shape and space through practical activity which builds on their understanding of their immediate environment. They begin to grasp mathematical language, using it to talk about their methods and explain their reasoning when solving problems.

The mathematics programmes of study and the National Numeracy Strategy *Framework for teaching mathematics* are fully aligned. The *Framework* provides a detailed basis for implementing the statutory requirements of the programme of study for key stage 1 in mathematics.

Building on the early learning goals
Pupils' prior experience of mathematics includes:

- counting and using numbers to at least 10 in familiar contexts
- recognising numerals 1 to 9
- talking about and creating simple patterns
- beginning to understand addition as combining two groups of objects and subtraction as 'taking away'
- describing the shape and size of solid and flat shapes
- using everyday words to describe position
- using early mathematical ideas to solve practical problems.

Note about sections
There is no separate section of the programme of study numbered Ma1 that corresponds to the first attainment target, **using and applying mathematics**. Teaching requirements relating to this attainment target are included within the other sections of the programme of study.

Programme of study: mathematics

Key stage 1

Knowledge, skills and understanding

Teaching should ensure that appropriate connections are made between the sections on **number** and **shape, space and measures**.

Ma2 Number

Using and applying number

1   Pupils should be taught to:

Problem solving

a   approach problems involving number, and data presented in a variety of forms, in order to identify what they need to do

b   develop flexible approaches to problem solving and look for ways to overcome difficulties

c   make decisions about which operations and problem-solving strategies to use

d   organise and check their work

Communicating

e   use the correct language, symbols and vocabulary associated with number and data

f   communicate in spoken, pictorial and written form, at first using informal language and recording, then mathematical language and symbols

Reasoning

g   present results in an organised way

h   understand a general statement and investigate whether particular cases match it

i   explain their methods and reasoning when solving problems involving number and data.

Numbers and the number system

2   Pupils should be taught to:

Counting

a   count reliably up to 20 objects at first and recognise that if the objects are rearranged the number stays the same; be familiar with the numbers 11 to 20; gradually extend counting to 100 and beyond

Number patterns and sequences

b   create and describe number patterns; explore and record patterns related to addition and subtraction, and then patterns of multiples of 2, 5 and 10 explaining the patterns and using them to make predictions; recognise sequences, including odd and even numbers to 30 then beyond; recognise the relationship between halving and doubling

The number system

c   read and write numbers to 20 at first and then to 100 or beyond; understand and use the vocabulary of comparing and ordering these numbers; recognise that the position of a digit gives its value and know what each digit represents, including zero as a place-holder; order a set of one- and two-digit numbers and position them on a number line and hundred-square; round any two-digit number to the nearest 10.

Calculations

3   Pupils should be taught to:

Number operations and the relationships between them

a   understand addition and use related vocabulary; recognise that addition can be done in any order; understand subtraction as both 'take away' and 'difference' and use the related vocabulary; recognise that subtraction is the inverse of addition; give the subtraction corresponding to an addition and vice versa; use the symbol '=' to represent equality; solve simple missing number problems [for example, 6 = 2 + □]

b   understand multiplication as repeated addition; understand that halving is the inverse of doubling and find one half and one quarter of shapes and small numbers of objects; begin to understand division as grouping (repeated subtraction); use vocabulary associated with multiplication and division

Mental methods

c   develop rapid recall of number facts: know addition and subtraction facts to 10 and use these to derive facts with totals to 20, know multiplication facts for the ×2 and ×10 multiplication tables and derive corresponding division facts, know doubles of numbers to 10 and halves of even numbers to 20

d   develop a range of mental methods for finding, from known facts, those that they cannot recall, including adding 10 to any single-digit number, then adding and subtracting a multiple of 10 to or from a two-digit number; develop a variety of methods for adding and subtracting, including making use of the facts that addition can be done in any order and that subtraction is the inverse of addition

e   carry out simple calculations of the form 40 + 30 = □, 40 + □ = 100, 56 − □ = 10; record calculations in a number sentence, using the symbols +, −, ×, ÷ and = correctly [for example, 7 + 2 = 9].

1e, 1f → **links to other subjects**
These requirements build on En1/1b–1c and En3/1c.

1f → **ICT opportunity**
Pupils could use ICT to communicate results using appropriate mathematical symbols.

Note for 1i
Explaining methods is an important foundation for reasoning and proof in later key stages.

Note for 5

This provides a basis for pupils' understanding of handling data in later key stages.

Solving numerical problems

4   Pupils should be taught to:

  a   choose sensible calculation methods to solve whole-number problems (including problems involving money or measures), drawing on their understanding of the operations

  b   check that their answers are reasonable and explain their methods or reasoning.

Processing, representing and interpreting data

5   Pupils should be taught to:

  a   solve a relevant problem by using simple lists, tables and charts to sort, classify and organise information

  b   discuss what they have done and explain their results.

Ma3 Shape, space and measures

Using and applying shape, space and measures

1 Pupils should be taught to:

Problem solving

a try different approaches and find ways of overcoming difficulties when solving shape and space problems

b select and use appropriate mathematical equipment when solving problems involving measures or measurement

c select and use appropriate equipment and materials when solving shape and space problems

Communicating

d use the correct language and vocabulary for shape, space and measures

Reasoning

e recognise simple spatial patterns and relationships and make predictions about them

f use mathematical communication and explanation skills.

Understanding patterns and properties of shape

2 Pupils should be taught to:

a describe properties of shapes that they can see or visualise using the related vocabulary

b observe, handle and describe common 2-D and 3-D shapes; name and describe the mathematical features of common 2-D and 3-D shapes, including triangles of various kinds, rectangles including squares, circles, cubes, cuboids, then hexagons, pentagons, cylinders, pyramids, cones and spheres

c create 2-D shapes and 3-D shapes

d recognise reflective symmetry in familiar 2-D shapes and patterns.

Understanding properties of position and movement

3 Pupils should be taught to:

a observe, visualise and describe positions, directions and movements using common words

b recognise movements in a straight line (translations) and rotations, and combine them in simple ways [for example, give instructions to get to the headteacher's office or for rotating a programmable toy]

c recognise right angles.

1b → ICT opportunity
Pupils could use both digital and analogue devices to measure weight or time.

1d → links to other subjects
This requirement builds on En1/1b.

Note for 1f
These skills are important foundations for geometrical reasoning and proof in later key stages.

Note for 4a
In the international system of units, kilogram (kg) is the unit of mass. In practice, mass is measured by weighing; scales measure or compare a force (a push or a pull). At key stage 1 it is acceptable to treat weight as synonymous with mass.

4b → ICT opportunity
Pupils could programme a toy to follow a path involving half- and quarter-turns.

Understanding measures

4 Pupils should be taught to:

a estimate the size of objects and order them by direct comparison using appropriate language; put familiar events in chronological order; compare and measure objects using uniform non-standard units [for example, a straw, wooden cubes], then with a standard unit of length (cm, m), weight (kg), capacity (l) [for example, 'longer or shorter than a metre rule', 'three-and-a-bit litre jugs']; compare the durations of events using a standard unit of time

b understand angle as a measure of turn using whole turns, half-turns and quarter-turns

c estimate, measure and weigh objects; choose and use simple measuring instruments, reading and interpreting numbers, and scales to the nearest labelled division.

Breadth of study

1 During the key stage, pupils should be taught the **Knowledge, skills and understanding** through:

a practical activity, exploration and discussion

b using mathematical ideas in practical activities, then recording these using objects, pictures, diagrams, words, numbers and symbols

c using mental images of numbers and their relationships to support the development of mental calculation strategies

d estimating, drawing and measuring in a range of practical contexts

e drawing inferences from data in practical activities

f exploring and using a variety of resources and materials, including ICT

g activities that encourage them to make connections between number work and other aspects of their work in mathematics.

Programme of study: mathematics

Key stage 2

Knowledge, skills and understanding

Teaching should ensure that appropriate connections are made between the sections on **number**, **shape, space and measures**, and **handling data**.

Ma2 Number

Using and applying number

1   Pupils should be taught to:

Problem solving

a   make connections in mathematics and appreciate the need to use numerical skills and knowledge when solving problems in other parts of the mathematics curriculum

b   break down a more complex problem or calculation into simpler steps before attempting a solution; identify the information needed to carry out the tasks

c   select and use appropriate mathematical equipment, including ICT

d   find different ways of approaching a problem in order to overcome any difficulties

e   make mental estimates of the answers to calculations; check results

Communicating

f   organise work and refine ways of recording

g   use notation diagrams and symbols correctly within a given problem

h   present and interpret solutions in the context of the problem

i   communicate mathematically, including the use of precise mathematical language

Reasoning

j   understand and investigate general statements [for example, 'there are four prime numbers less than 10', 'wrist size is half neck size']

k   search for pattern in their results; develop logical thinking and explain their reasoning.

Numbers and the number system

2   Pupils should be taught to:

Counting

a   count on and back in tens or hundreds from any two- or three-digit number; recognise and continue number sequences formed by counting on or back in steps of constant size from any integer, extending to negative integers when counting back

During key stage 2 pupils use the number system more confidently. They move from counting reliably to calculating fluently with all four number operations. They always try to tackle a problem with mental methods before using any other approach. Pupils explore features of shape and space and develop their measuring skills in a range of contexts. They discuss and present their methods and reasoning using a wider range of mathematical language, diagrams and charts.

The mathematics programmes of study and the National Numeracy Strategy *Framework for teaching mathematics* are fully aligned. The *Framework* provides a detailed basis for implementing the statutory requirements of the programme of study for key stage 2 in mathematics.

Note about sections
There is no separate section of the programme of study numbered Ma1 that corresponds to the first attainment target, **using and applying mathematics**. Teaching requirements relating to this attainment target are included within the other sections of the programme of study.

1f → links to other subjects
This requirement builds on En3/1a, 1e.

1g → links to other subjects
This requirement builds on En1/1a, 1d.

Number patterns and sequences

b   recognise and describe number patterns, including two- and three-digit multiples of 2, 5 or 10, recognising their patterns and using these to make predictions; make general statements, using words to describe a functional relationship, and test these; recognise prime numbers to 20 and square numbers up to 10 × 10; find factor pairs and all the prime factors of any two-digit integer

Integers

c   read, write and order whole numbers, recognising that the position of a digit gives its value; use correctly the symbols <, >, =; multiply and divide any integer by 10 or 100 then extend to multiplying and dividing by 1000; round integers to the nearest 10 or 100 and then 1000; order a set of negative integers, explaining methods and reasoning; multiply and divide decimals by 10 or 100

Fractions, percentages and ratio

d   understand unit fractions [for example, $\frac{1}{3}$ or $\frac{1}{8}$] then fractions that are several parts of one whole [for example, $\frac{2}{3}$ or $\frac{5}{8}$], locate them on a number line and use them to find fractions of shapes and quantities

e   understand simple equivalent fractions and simplify fractions by cancelling common factors; compare and order simple fractions by converting them to fractions with a common denominator, explaining their methods and reasoning

f   recognise the equivalence between the decimal and fraction forms of one half, quarters, tenths and hundredths; understand that 'percentage' means the 'number of parts per 100' and that it can be used for comparisons; find percentages of whole number quantities, using a calculator where appropriate

g   recognise approximate proportions of a whole and use simple fractions and percentages to describe them, explaining their methods and reasoning

h   solve simple problems involving ratio and direct proportion

Decimals

i   understand and use decimal notation for tenths and hundredths in context [for example, order amounts of money, round a sum of money to the nearest £, convert a length such as 1.36 metres to centimetres and vice versa]; locate on a number line, and order, a set of numbers or measurements; then recognise thousandths (only in metric measurements)

j   round a number with one or two decimal places to the nearest integer or tenth; convert between centimetres and millimetres or metres, then between millimetres and metres, and metres and kilometres, explaining methods and reasoning.

Calculations

3   Pupils should be taught to:

Number operations and the relationships between them

a   develop further their understanding of the four number operations and the relationships between them including inverses; use the related vocabulary; choose suitable number operations to solve a given problem, and recognise similar problems to which they apply

b   find remainders after division, then express a quotient as a fraction or decimal; round up or down after division, depending on the context

c   understand the use of brackets to determine the order of operations; understand why the commutative, associative and distributive laws apply to addition and multiplication and how they can be used to do mental and written calculations more efficiently

Mental methods

d   recall all addition and subtraction facts for each number to 20

e   work out what they need to add to any two-digit number to make 100, then add or subtract any pair of two-digit whole numbers; handle particular cases of three-digit and four-digit additions and subtractions by using compensation or other methods [for example, $3000 - 1997$, $4560 + 998$]

f   recall multiplication facts to 10×10 and use them to derive quickly the corresponding division facts

g   double and halve any two-digit number

h   multiply and divide, at first in the range 1 to 100 [for example, 27×3, $65 \div 5$], then for particular cases of larger numbers by using factors, distribution or other methods

Written methods

i   use written methods to add and subtract positive integers less than 1000, then up to 10000, then add and subtract numbers involving decimals; use approximations and other strategies to check that their answers are reasonable

j   use written methods for short multiplication and division by a single-digit integer of two-digit then three-digit then four-digit integers, then of numbers with decimals; then use long multiplication, at first for two-digit by two-digit integer calculations, then for three-digit by two-digit calculations; extend division to informal methods of dividing by a two-digit divisor [for example, $64 \div 16$]; use approximations and other strategies to check that their answers are reasonable

Note for 3c
Pupils do not need to know the names of these laws.

Note for 3i, 3j
Pupils are expected to use mental methods if the calculations are suitable.

4d → ICT opportunity
Pupils could construct and use a formula
to transform one list of data to another.

Calculator methods

k use a calculator for calculations involving several digits, including decimals; use a calculator to solve number problems [for example, $4 \square \times 7 = 343$]; know how to enter and interpret money calculations and fractions; know how to select the correct key sequence for calculations with more than one operation [for example, $56 \times (87 - 48)$].

Solving numerical problems

4 Pupils should be taught to:

a choose, use and combine any of the four number operations to solve word problems involving numbers in 'real life', money or measures of length, mass, capacity or time, then perimeter and area

b choose and use an appropriate way to calculate and explain their methods and reasoning

c estimate answers by approximating and checking that their results are reasonable by thinking about the context of the problem, and where necessary checking accuracy [for example, by using the inverse operation, by repeating the calculation in a different order]

d recognise, represent and interpret simple number relationships, constructing and using formulae in words then symbols [for example, $c = 15n$ is the cost, in pence, of n articles at 15p each]

e read and plot coordinates in the first quadrant, then in all four quadrants [for example, plot the vertices of a rectangle, or a graph of the multiples of 3].

Ma3 Shape, space and measures

Using and applying shape, space and measures

1 Pupils should be taught to:

Problem solving

a recognise the need for standard units of measurement

b select and use appropriate calculation skills to solve geometrical problems

c approach spatial problems flexibly, including trying alternative approaches to overcome difficulties

d use checking procedures to confirm that their results of geometrical problems are reasonable

Communicating

e organise work and record or represent it in a variety of ways when presenting solutions to geometrical problems

f use geometrical notation and symbols correctly

g present and interpret solutions to problems

Reasoning

h use mathematical reasoning to explain features of shape and space.

Understanding properties of shape

2 Pupils should be taught to:

a recognise right angles, perpendicular and parallel lines; know that angles are measured in degrees and that one whole turn is 360 degrees and angles at a point total 360 degrees, then recognise that angles at a point on a straight line total 180 degrees; know that the sum of the angles of a triangle is 180 degrees

b visualise and describe 2-D and 3-D shapes and the way they behave, making more precise use of geometrical language, especially that of triangles, quadrilaterals, and prisms and pyramids of various kinds; recognise when shapes are identical

c make and draw with increasing accuracy 2-D and 3-D shapes and patterns; recognise reflective symmetry in regular polygons; recognise their geometrical features and properties including angles, faces, pairs of parallel lines and symmetry, and use these to classify shapes and solve problems

d visualise 3-D shapes from 2-D drawings.

Understanding properties of position and movement

3 Pupils should be taught to:

a visualise and describe movements using appropriate language

b transform objects in practical situations; transform images using ICT; visualise and predict the position of a shape following a rotation, reflection or translation

1c → ICT opportunity
Pupils could use software to create repeating patterns, such as tessellations.

1e, 1g → link to other subjects
These requirements build on En1/1a, 1c and En3/1a, 1e.

2c → ICT opportunity
Pupils could use object drawing software to plan alternative layouts for a room.

Note for 4a

In the international system of units, kilogram (kg) is the unit of mass. In practice, mass is measured by weighing; scales measure or compare a force (a push or a pull). Initially it is acceptable to treat weight as synonymous with mass but later in key stage 2 pupils will learn that the unit of weight (as type of force) is the newton.

c identify and draw 2-D shapes in different orientations on grids; locate and draw shapes using coordinates in the first quadrant, then in all four quadrants [for example, use coordinates to locate position in a computer game].

Understanding measures

4 Pupils should be taught to:

a recognise the need for standard units of length, mass and capacity, choose which ones are suitable for a task, and use them to make sensible estimates in everyday situations; convert one metric unit to another [for example, convert 3.17kg to 3170g]; know the rough metric equivalents of imperial units still in daily use

b recognise that measurement is approximate; choose and use suitable measuring instruments for a task; interpret numbers and read scales with increasing accuracy; record measurements using decimal notation

c recognise angles as greater or less than a right angle or half-turn, estimate their size and order them; measure and draw acute, obtuse and right angles to the nearest degree

d read the time from analogue and digital 12- and 24-hour clocks; use units of time – seconds, minutes, hours, days, weeks – and know the relationship between them

e find perimeters of simple shapes; find areas of rectangles using the formula, understanding its connection to counting squares and how it extends this approach; calculate the perimeter and area of shapes composed of rectangles.

Ma4 Handling data

Using and applying handling data

1   Pupils should be taught to:

Problem solving

a   select and use handling data skills when solving problems in other areas
    of the curriculum, in particular science

b   approach problems flexibly, including trying alternative approaches
    to overcome any difficulties

c   identify the data necessary to solve a given problem

d   select and use appropriate calculation skills to solve problems involving data

e   check results and ensure that solutions are reasonable in the context of
    the problem

Communicating

f   decide how best to organise and present findings

g   use the precise mathematical language and vocabulary for handling data

Reasoning

h   explain and justify their methods and reasoning.

Processing, representing and interpreting data

2   Pupils should be taught to:

a   solve problems involving data

b   interpret tables, lists and charts used in everyday life; construct and interpret
    frequency tables, including tables for grouped discrete data

c   represent and interpret discrete data using graphs and diagrams, including
    pictograms, bar charts and line graphs, then interpret a wider range
    of graphs and diagrams, using ICT where appropriate

d   know that mode is a measure of average and that range is a measure
    of spread, and to use both ideas to describe data sets

e   recognise the difference between discrete and continuous data

f   draw conclusions from statistics and graphs and recognise when information
    is presented in a misleading way; explore doubt and certainty and develop
    an understanding of probability through classroom situations; discuss
    events using a vocabulary that includes the words 'equally likely', 'fair',
    'unfair', 'certain'.

1f → links to other subjects
This requirement builds on En3/1a, 1e.

1g → links to other subjects
This requirement builds on En1/1a, 1c.

Breadth of study

1   During the key stage, pupils should be taught the **Knowledge, skills and understanding** through:

  a   activities that extend their understanding of the number system to include integers, fractions and decimals

  b   approximating and estimating more systematically in their work in mathematics

  c   using patterns and relationships to explore simple algebraic ideas

  d   applying their measuring skills in a range of contexts

  e   drawing inferences from data in practical activities, and recognising the difference between meaningful and misleading representations of data

  f   exploring and using a variety of resources and materials, including ICT

  g   activities in which pupils decide when the use of calculators is appropriate and then use them effectively

  h   using mathematics in their work in other subjects.

Programme of study: mathematics

Key stage 3

Knowledge, skills and understanding

Teaching should ensure that appropriate connections are made between the sections on **number and algebra**, **shape, space and measures**, and **handling data**.

Ma2 Number and algebra

Using and applying number and algebra

1 Pupils should be taught to:

Problem solving

a explore connections in mathematics to develop flexible approaches to increasingly demanding problems; select appropriate strategies to use for numerical or algebraic problems

b break down a complex calculation into simpler steps before attempting to solve it

c use alternative approaches to overcome difficulties and evaluate the effectiveness of their strategies

d select efficient techniques for numerical calculation and algebraic manipulation

e make mental estimates of the answers to calculations; use checking procedures to monitor the accuracy of their results

Communicating

f represent problems and solutions in algebraic or graphical forms; move from one form of representation to another to get different perspectives on the problem; present and interpret solutions in the context of the original problem

g develop correct and consistent use of notation, symbols and diagrams when solving problems

h examine critically, improve, then justify their choice of mathematical presentation; present a concise, reasoned argument

Reasoning

i explore, identify, and use pattern and symmetry in algebraic contexts, investigating whether particular cases can be generalised further and understanding the importance of a counter-example; identify exceptional cases when solving problems; make conjectures and check them for new cases

j show step-by-step deduction in solving a problem; explain and justify how they arrived at a conclusion

k distinguish between a practical demonstration and a proof

l recognise the importance of assumptions when deducing results; recognise the limitations of any assumptions that are made and the effect that varying the assumptions may have on the solution to a problem.

During key stage 3 pupils take increasing responsibility for planning and executing their work. They extend their calculating skills to fractions, percentages and decimals, and begin to understand the importance of proportional reasoning. They are beginning to use algebraic techniques and symbols with confidence. They generate and solve simple equations and study linear functions and their corresponding graphs. They begin to use deduction to manipulate algebraic expressions. Pupils progress from a simple understanding of the features of shape and space to using definitions and reasoning to understand geometrical objects. As they encounter simple algebraic and geometric proofs, they begin to understand reasoned arguments. They communicate mathematics in speech and a variety of written forms, explaining their reasoning to others. They study handling data through practical activities and are introduced to a quantitative approach to probability. Pupils work with increasing confidence and flexibility to solve unfamiliar problems. They develop positive attitudes towards mathematics and increasingly make connections between different aspects of mathematics.

Note
This programme of study covers the attainment range for this key stage. Teachers are expected to plan work drawing on all the numbered sub-sections of the programme of study. For some groups of pupils, all or part of particular lettered paragraphs may not be appropriate.

Note about sections
There is no separate section of the programme of study numbered Ma1 that corresponds to the first attainment target, **using and applying mathematics**. Teaching requirements relating to this attainment target are included within the other sections of the programme of study.

1f → links to other subjects
This requirement builds on En1/1d and En3/1n.

1h → links to other subjects
This requirement builds on En1/1e, 3b and En3/1f, 1i.

Numbers and the number system

2   Pupils should be taught to:

Integers

a   use their previous understanding of integers and place value to deal with arbitrarily large positive numbers and round them to a given power of 10; understand and use negative numbers, both as positions and translations on a number line; order integers; use the concepts and vocabulary of factor (divisor), multiple, common factor, highest common factor, least common multiple, prime number and prime factor decomposition

Powers and roots

b   use the terms square, positive and negative square root (knowing that the square root sign denotes the positive square root), cube, cube root; use index notation for small integer powers and index laws for multiplication and division of positive integer powers

Fractions

c   use fraction notation; understand equivalent fractions, simplifying a fraction by cancelling all common factors; order fractions by rewriting them with a common denominator

Decimals

d   use decimal notation and recognise that each terminating decimal is a fraction [for example, $0.137 = \frac{137}{1000}$]; order decimals

Percentages

e   understand that 'percentage' means 'number of parts per 100' and use this to compare proportions; interpret percentage as the operator 'so many hundredths of' [for example, 10% means 10 parts per 100 and 15% of Y means $\frac{15}{100} \times Y$]

Ratio and proportion

f   use ratio notation, including reduction to its simplest form and its various links to fraction notation

g   recognise where fractions or percentages are needed to compare proportions; identify problems that call for proportional reasoning, and choose the correct numbers to take as 100%, or as a whole.

Calculations

3 Pupils should be taught to:

Number operations and the relationships between them

a add, subtract, multiply and divide integers and then any number; multiply or divide any number by powers of 10, and any positive number by a number between 0 and 1; find the prime factor decomposition of positive integers [for example, $8000 = 2^6 \times 5^3$]

b use brackets and the hierarchy of operations; know how to use the commutative, associative and distributive laws to do mental and written calculations more efficiently

c calculate a given fraction of a given quantity, expressing the answer as a fraction; express a given number as a fraction of another; add and subtract fractions by writing them with a common denominator; perform short division to convert a simple fraction to a decimal

d understand and use unit fractions as multiplicative inverses [for example, by thinking of multiplication by $\frac{1}{5}$ as division by 5, or multiplication by $\frac{6}{7}$ as multiplication by 6 followed by division by 7 (or vice versa)]; multiply and divide a given fraction by an integer, by a unit fraction and by a general fraction

e convert simple fractions of a whole to percentages of the whole and vice versa, then understand the multiplicative nature of percentages as operators [for example, 20% discount on £150 gives a total calculated as £(0.8×150)]

f divide a quantity in a given ratio [for example, share £15 in the ratio 1:2]

Mental methods

g recall all positive integer complements to 100 [for example, $37 + 63 = 100$]; recall all multiplication facts to 10×10, and use them to derive quickly the corresponding division facts; recall the cubes of 2, 3, 4, 5 and 10, and the fraction-to-decimal conversion of familiar simple fractions [for example, $\frac{1}{2}, \frac{1}{4}, \frac{1}{5}, \frac{1}{10}, \frac{1}{100}, \frac{1}{3}, \frac{2}{3}, \frac{1}{8}$]

h round to the nearest integer and to one significant figure; estimate answers to problems involving decimals

i develop a range of strategies for mental calculation; derive unknown facts from those they know [for example, estimate $\sqrt{85}$]; add and subtract mentally numbers with up to two decimal places [for example, $13.76 - 5.21$, $20.08 + 12.4$]; multiply and divide numbers with no more than one decimal digit [for example, 14.3×4, $56.7 \div 7$], using factorisation when possible

Note for 3b
Pupils do not need to know the names of these laws.

Written methods

j   use standard column procedures for addition and subtraction of integers and decimals

k   use standard column procedures for multiplication of integers and decimals, understanding where to position the decimal point by considering what happens if they multiply equivalent fractions [for example, $0.6 \times 0.7 = 0.42$ since $\frac{6}{10} \times \frac{7}{10} = \frac{42}{100} = 0.42$]; solve a problem involving division by a decimal by transforming it to a problem involving division by an integer

l   use efficient methods to calculate with fractions, including cancelling common factors before carrying out the calculation, recognising that, in many cases, only a fraction can express the exact answer

m solve simple percentage problems, including increase and decrease [for example, simple interest, VAT, discounts, pay rises, annual rate of inflation, income tax, discounts]

n   solve word problems about ratio and proportion, including using informal strategies and the unitary method of solution [for example, given that m identical items cost £y, then one item costs £$\frac{y}{m}$ and n items cost £$(n \times \frac{y}{m})$, the number of items that can be bought for £z is $z \times \frac{m}{y}$]

Calculator methods

o   use calculators effectively and efficiently: know how to enter complex calculations using brackets [for example, for negative numbers, or the division of more than one term], know how to enter a range of calculations, including those involving measures [for example, time calculations in which fractions of an hour need to be entered as fractions or decimals]

p   use the function keys for reciprocals, squares, square roots, powers, fractions (and how to enter a fraction as a decimal); use the constant key

q   understand the calculator display, interpreting it correctly [for example, in money calculations, and when the display has been rounded by the calculator], and knowing not to round during the intermediate steps of a calculation.

Solving numerical problems

4   Pupils should be taught to:

a   draw on their knowledge of the operations and the relationships between them, and of simple integer powers and their corresponding roots, to solve problems involving ratio and proportion, a range of measures and compound measures, metric units, and conversion between metric and common imperial units, set in a variety of contexts b   select appropriate operations, methods and strategies to solve number problems, including trial and improvement where a more efficient method to find the solution is not obvious

c   use a variety of checking procedures, including working the problem backwards, and considering whether a result is of the right order of magnitude

d   give solutions in the context of the problem to an appropriate degree of accuracy, recognising limitations on the accuracy of data and measurements.

Equations, formulae and identities

5   Pupils should be taught to:

Use of symbols

a   distinguish the different roles played by letter symbols in algebra, knowing that letter symbols represent definite unknown numbers in equations [for example, $x^3 + 1 = 65$], defined quantities or variables in formulae [for example, $V = IR$], general, unspecified and independent numbers in identities [for example, $3x + 2x = 5x$, or $3(a + b) = 3a + 3b$, or $(x + 1)(x - 1)$ $= x^2 - 1$] and in functions they define new expressions or quantities by referring to known quantities [for example, $y = 2 - 7x$]

b   understand that the transformation of algebraic expressions obeys and generalises the rules of arithmetic; simplify or transform algebraic expressions by collecting like terms [for example, $x^2 + 3x + 5 - 4x + 2x^2 = 3x^2 - x + 5$], by multiplying a single term over a bracket, by taking out single term common factors [for example, $x^2 + x = x(x + 1)$], and by expanding the product of two linear expressions including squaring a linear expression [for example, $(x + 1)^2 = x^2 + 2x + 1$, $(x - 3)(x + 2) = x^2 - x - 6$]; distinguish in meaning between the words 'equation', 'formula', 'identity' and 'expression'

Index notation

c   use index notation for simple integer powers, and simple instances of index laws; substitute positive and negative numbers into expressions such as $3x^2 + 4$ and $2x^3$

Equations

d   set up simple equations [for example, find the angle a in a triangle with angles a, $a + 10$, $a + 20$]; solve simple equations [for example, $5x = 7$, $3(2x + 1) = 8$, $2(1 - x) = 6 (2 + x)$, $4x^2 = 36$, $3 = \frac{12}{x}$], by using inverse operations or by transforming both sides in the same way

5f → ICT opportunity
Pupils could use a spreadsheet to construct
formulae to model situations.

Linear equations

e solve linear equations, with integer coefficients, in which the unknown
appears on either side or on both sides of the equation; solve linear
equations that require prior simplification of brackets, including those
that have negative signs occurring anywhere in the equation, and those
with a negative solution

Formulae

f use formulae from mathematics and other subjects [for example, formulae
for the area of a triangle, the area enclosed by a circle,
density = mass/volume]; substitute numbers into a formula; derive a formula
and change its subject [for example, convert temperatures between degrees
Fahrenheit and degrees Celsius, find the perimeter of a rectangle given its
area A and the length *l* of one side]

Direct proportion

g set up and use equations to solve word and other problems involving direct
proportion, and relate their algebraic solutions to graphical representations
of the equations

Simultaneous linear equations

h link a graphical representation of an equation to its algebraic solution; find
an approximate solution of a pair of linear simultaneous equations by
graphical methods, then find the exact solution by eliminating one variable;
consider the graphs of cases that have no solution, or an infinite number
of solutions

Inequalities

i solve simple linear inequalities in one variable, and represent the solution
set on a number line

Numerical methods

j use systematic trial and improvement methods with ICT tools to find
approximate solutions of equations where there is no simple analytical
method [for example, $x^3 + x = 100$].

Sequences, functions and graphs

6 Pupils should be taught to:

Sequences

a generate common integer sequences (including sequences of odd or even
integers, squared integers, powers of 2, powers of 10, triangular numbers)

b find the first terms of a sequence given a rule arising naturally from a
context [for example, the number of ways of paying in pence using only 1p
and 2p coins, or from a regularly increasing spatial pattern]; find the rule
(and express it in words) for the *n*th term of a sequence

c   generate terms of a sequence using term-to-term and position-to-term definitions of the sequence; use linear expressions to describe the nth term of an arithmetic sequence, justifying its form by referring to the activity or context from which it was generated

Functions

d   express simple functions, at first in words and then in symbols; explore the properties of simple polynomial functions

e   use the conventions for coordinates in the plane; plot points in all four quadrants; recognise (when values are given for m and c) that equations of the form $y = mx + c$ correspond to straight-line graphs in the coordinate plane; plot graphs of functions in which y is given explicitly in terms of x [for example, $y = 2x + 3$], or implicitly [for example, $x + y = 7$]

f   construct linear functions arising from real-life problems and plot their corresponding graphs; discuss and interpret graphs arising from real situations [for example, distance–time graph for an object moving with constant speed]

g   generate points and plot graphs of simple quadratic and cubic functions [for example, $y = x^2$, $y = 3x^2 + 4$, $y = x^3$]

Gradients

h   find the gradient of lines given by equations of the form $y = mx + c$ (when values are given for m and c); investigate the gradients of parallel lines and lines perpendicular to these lines [for example, knowing that $y = 5x$ and $y = 5x - 4$ represent parallel lines, each with gradient 5 and that the graph of any line perpendicular to these lines has gradient $-\frac{1}{5}$].

6g → ICT opportunity
Pupils could use a spreadsheet to generate points and plot graphs.

1d → links to other subjects
This requirement builds on En1/3b and En2/1a.

1e → links to other subjects
This requirement builds on En1/1d and En3/1f.

1f → links to other subjects
This requirement builds on En3/1f.

1g → links to other subjects
This requirement builds on En1/1e, 3b and En3/1i, 1n.

Ma3 Shape, space and measures

Using and applying shape, space and measures

1 Pupils should be taught to:

Problem solving

a select problem-solving strategies and resources, including ICT, to use in geometrical work, and monitor their effectiveness

b select and combine known facts and problem-solving strategies to solve complex problems

c identify what further information is needed to solve a problem; break complex problems down into a series of tasks

Communication

d interpret, discuss and synthesise geometrical information presented in a variety of forms

e communicate mathematically, making use of geometrical diagrams and related explanatory text

f use precise language and exact methods to analyse geometrical configurations

g review and justify their choices of mathematical presentation

Reasoning

h distinguish between practical demonstration, proof, conventions, facts, definitions and derived properties

i explain and justify inferences and deductions using mathematical reasoning

j explore connections in geometry; pose conditional constraints of the type 'If … then …'; and ask questions 'What if …?' or 'Why?'

k show step-by-step deduction in solving a geometrical problem

l state constraints and give starting points when making deductions

m recognise the limitations of any assumptions that are made; understand the effects that varying the assumptions may have on the solution

n identify exceptional cases when solving geometrical problems.

Geometrical reasoning

2 Pupils should be taught to:

Angles

a recall and use properties of angles at a point, angles on a straight line (including right angles), perpendicular lines, and opposite angles at a vertex

b distinguish between acute, obtuse, reflex and right angles; estimate the size of an angle in degrees

Properties of triangles and other rectilinear shapes

c use parallel lines, alternate angles and corresponding angles; understand the properties of parallelograms and a proof that the angle sum of a triangle is 180 degrees; understand a proof that the exterior angle of a triangle is equal to the sum of the interior angles at the other two vertices

d   use angle properties of equilateral, isosceles and right-angled triangles; understand congruence, recognising when two triangles are congruent; explain why the angle sum of any quadrilateral is 360 degrees

e   use their knowledge of rectangles, parallelograms and triangles to deduce formulae for the area of a parallelogram, and a triangle, from the formula for the area of a rectangle

f   recall the essential properties of special types of quadrilateral, including square, rectangle, parallelogram, trapezium and rhombus; classify quadrilaterals by their geometric properties

g   calculate and use the sums of the interior and exterior angles of quadrilaterals, pentagons and hexagons; calculate and use the angles of regular polygons

h   understand, recall and use Pythagoras' theorem

Properties of circles

i   recall the definition of a circle and the meaning of related terms, including centre, radius, chord, diameter, circumference, tangent, arc, sector and segment; understand that the tangent at any point on a circle is perpendicular to the radius at that point; explain why the perpendicular from the centre to a chord bisects the chord; understand that inscribed regular polygons can be constructed by equal division of a circle

3-D shapes

j   explore the geometry of cuboids (including cubes), and shapes made from cuboids

k   use 2-D representations of 3-D shapes and analyse 3-D shapes through 2-D projections and cross-sections, including plan and elevation.

Transformations and coordinates

3   Pupils should be taught to:

Specifying transformations

a   understand that rotations are specified by a centre and an (anticlockwise) angle; use right angles, fractions of a turn or degrees to measure the angle of rotation; understand that reflections are specified by a mirror line, translations by a distance and direction, and enlargements by a centre and positive scale factor

Properties of transformations

b   recognise and visualise rotations, reflections and translations, including reflection symmetry of 2-D and 3-D shapes, and rotation symmetry of 2-D shapes; transform 2-D shapes by translation, rotation and reflection, recognising that these transformations preserve length and angle, so that any figure is congruent to its image under any of these transformations

Note for 3d
Enlargement of triangles is fundamental
to work in trigonometry in the higher
programme of study for key stage 4 Ma3/2g.

c   recognise, visualise and construct enlargements of objects using positive
integer scale factors greater than one, then positive scale factors less than
one; understand from this that any two circles and any two squares are
mathematically similar, while, in general, two rectangles are not

d   recognise that enlargements preserve angle but not length; identify the scale
factor of an enlargement as the ratio of the lengths of any two
corresponding line segments and apply this to triangles; understand the
implications of enlargement for perimeter; use and interpret maps and
scale drawings; understand the implications of enlargement for area and
for volume

Coordinates

e   understand that one coordinate identifies a point on a number line, two
coordinates identify a point in a plane and three coordinates identify a point
in space, using the terms '1-D', '2-D' and '3-D'; use axes and coordinates
to specify points in all four quadrants; locate points with given coordinates;
find the coordinates of points identified by geometrical information [for
example, find the coordinates of the fourth vertex of a parallelogram with
vertices at (2, 1) (–7, 3) and (5, 6)]; find the coordinates of the midpoint
of the line segment AB, given points A and B, then calculate the length AB.

Measures and construction

4   Pupils should be taught to:

Measures

a   interpret scales on a range of measuring instruments, including those for
time and mass; know that measurements using real numbers depend on
the choice of unit; recognise that measurements given to the nearest whole
unit may be inaccurate by up to one half in either direction; convert
measurements from one unit to another; know rough metric equivalents
of pounds, feet, miles, pints and gallons; make sensible estimates of a range
of measures in everyday settings

b   understand angle measure, using the associated language [for example,
use bearings to specify direction]

c   understand and use compound measures, including speed and density

Construction

d   measure and draw lines to the nearest millimetre, and angles to the nearest
degree; draw triangles and other 2-D shapes using a ruler and protractor,
given information about their side lengths and angles; understand, from
their experience of constructing them, that triangles satisfying SSS, SAS,
ASA and RHS are unique, but SSA triangles are not; construct cubes, regular
tetrahedra, square-based pyramids and other 3-D shapes from given information

e   use straight edge and compasses to do standard constructions, including an equilateral triangle with a given side, the midpoint and perpendicular bisector of a line segment, the perpendicular from a point to a line, the perpendicular from a point on a line, and the bisector of an angle

Mensuration

f   find areas of rectangles, recalling the formula, understanding the connection to counting squares and how it extends this approach; recall and use the formulae for the area of a parallelogram and a triangle; find the surface area of simple shapes using the area formulae for triangles and rectangles; calculate perimeters and areas of shapes made from triangles and rectangles

g   find volumes of cuboids, recalling the formula and understanding the connection to counting cubes and how it extends this approach; calculate volumes of right prisms and of shapes made from cubes and cuboids

h   find circumferences of circles and areas enclosed by circles, recalling relevant formulae

i   convert between area measures, including cm^2 and m^2, and volume measures, including cm^3 and m^3

Loci

j   find loci, both by reasoning and by using ICT to produce shapes and paths [for example, equilateral triangles].

1e → **links to other subjects**
This requirement builds on En1/3b
and En2/1a.

1f → **ICT opportunity**
Pupils could use presentation software
to communicate their findings and display
the data.

1f → **links to other subjects**
This requirement builds on En1/1d
and En3/1f.

1g → **links to other subjects**
This requirement builds on En1/1e,
3b and En3/1i, 1n.

Ma4 Handling data

Using and applying handling data

1   Pupils should be taught to:

Problem solving

a   carry out each of the four aspects of the handling data cycle to solve problems:

   i   specify the problem and plan: formulate questions in terms of the data needed, and consider what inferences can be drawn from the data; decide what data to collect (including sample size and data format) and what statistical analysis is needed

   ii   collect data from a variety of suitable sources, including experiments and surveys, and primary and secondary sources

   iii   process and represent the data: turn the raw data into usable information that gives insight into the problem

   iv   interpret and discuss the data: answer the initial question by drawing conclusions from the data

b   identify what further information is required to pursue a particular line of enquiry

c   select and organise the appropriate mathematics and resources to use for a task

d   review progress as they work; check and evaluate solutions

Communicating

e   interpret, discuss and synthesise information presented in a variety of forms

f   communicate mathematically, making use of diagrams and related explanatory text

g   examine critically, and justify, their choice of mathematical presentation of problems involving data

Reasoning

h   apply mathematical reasoning, explaining and justifying inferences and deductions

i   explore connections in mathematics and look for cause and effect when analysing data

j   recognise the limitations of any assumptions, and the effects that varying the assumptions could have on conclusions drawn from the data analysis.

Specifying the problem and planning

2   Pupils should be taught to:

a   see that random processes are unpredictable

b   identify questions that can be addressed by statistical methods

c   discuss how data relate to a problem; identify possible sources of bias and plan to minimise it

5c → ICT opportunity
Pupils could use databases to present
their findings.

  d   identify which primary data they need to collect and in what format
      (including grouped data, considering appropriate equal class intervals)

  e   design an experiment or survey; decide what secondary data to use.

Collecting data

3 Pupils should be taught to:

  a   design and use data-collection sheets for grouped discrete and continuous
      data; collect data using various methods including observation, controlled
      experiment, data logging, questionnaires and surveys

  b   gather data from secondary sources, including printed tables and lists
      from ICT-based sources

  c   design and use two-way tables for discrete and grouped data.

Processing and representing data

4 Pupils should be taught to:

  a   draw and produce, using paper and ICT, pie charts for categorical data and
      diagrams for continuous data, including line graphs for time series, scatter
      graphs, frequency diagrams and stem-and-leaf diagrams

  b   calculate mean, range and median of small data sets with discrete then
      continuous data; identify the modal class for grouped data

  c   understand and use the probability scale

  d   understand and use estimates or measures of probability from theoretical
      models, including equally likely outcomes, or from relative frequency

  e   list all outcomes for single events, and for two successive events, in a
      systematic way

  f   identify different mutually exclusive outcomes and know that the sum
      of the probabilities of all these outcomes is 1

  g   find the median for large data sets and calculate an estimate of the mean
      for large data sets with grouped data

  h   draw lines of best fit by eye, understanding what these represent.

Interpreting and discussing results

5 Pupils should be taught to:

  a   relate summarised data to the initial questions

  b   interpret a wide range of graphs and diagrams and draw conclusions

  c   look at data to find patterns and exceptions

  d   compare distributions and make inferences, using the shapes of distributions
      and measures of average and range

  e   evaluate and check results, answer questions, and modify their approach
      if necessary

  f   have a basic understanding of correlation

  g   use lines of best fit

h   use the vocabulary of probability in interpreting results involving uncertainty and prediction

i   compare experimental data and theoretical probabilities

j   understand that if they repeat an experiment, they may – and usually will – get different outcomes, and that increasing sample size generally leads to better estimates of probability and population characteristics.

Breadth of study

1   During the key stage, pupils should be taught the **Knowledge, skills and understanding** through:

    a   activities that ensure they become familiar with and confident using standard procedures for a range of problems, including ratio and proportion

    b   activities that enable them to understand that algebra is an extension of number

    c   solving familiar and unfamiliar problems, including multi-step problems, in a range of numerical, algebraic and graphical contexts and in open-ended and closed form

    d   activities that develop short chains of deductive reasoning and concepts of proof in algebra and geometry

    e   activities focused on geometrical definitions in which they do practical work with geometrical objects to develop their ability to visualise these objects and work with them mentally

    f   practical work in which they draw inferences from data and consider how statistics are used in real life to make informed decisions

    g   a sequence of activities that address increasingly demanding statistical problems

    h   tasks focused on using appropriate ICT [for example, spreadsheets, databases, geometry or graphic packages], using calculators correctly and efficiently, and knowing when it is not appropriate to use a particular form of technology.

Programme of study: mathematics foundation

Key stage 4

Knowledge, skills and understanding

Teaching should ensure that appropriate connections are made between the sections on **number and algebra**, **shape, space and measures**, and **handling data**.

Ma2 Number and algebra

Using and applying number and algebra

1   Pupils should be taught to:

Problem solving

a   select and use suitable problem-solving strategies and efficient techniques to solve numerical and algebraic problems

b   break down a complex calculation into simpler steps before attempting to solve it

c   use algebra to formulate and solve a simple problem – identifying the variable, setting up an equation, solving the equation and interpreting the solution in the context of the problem

d   make mental estimates of the answers to calculations; use checking procedures, including use of inverse operations; work to stated levels of accuracy

Communicating

e   interpret and discuss numerical and algebraic information presented in a variety of forms

f   use notation and symbols correctly and consistently within a given problem

g   use a range of strategies to create numerical, algebraic or graphical representations of a problem and its solution; move from one form of representation to another to get different perspectives on the problem

h   present and interpret solutions in the context of the original problem

i   review and justify their choice of mathematical presentation

Reasoning

j   explore, identify, and use pattern and symmetry in algebraic contexts [for example, using simple codes that substitute numbers for letters], investigating whether particular cases can be generalised further, and understanding the importance of a counter-example; identify exceptional cases when solving problems

k   show step-by-step deduction in solving a problem

l   distinguish between a practical demonstration and a proof

m   recognise the importance of assumptions when deducing results; recognise the limitations of any assumptions that are made and the effect that varying the assumptions may have on the solution to a problem.

During key stage 4 (foundation) pupils consolidate their understanding of basic mathematics, which will help them to tackle unfamiliar problems in the workplace and everyday life and develop the knowledge and skills they need in the future. They become more fluent in making connections between different areas of mathematics and its application in the world around them. They become increasingly proficient in calculating fractions, percentages and decimals, and use proportional reasoning in simple contexts. Building on their understanding of numbers, they make generalisations using letters, manipulate simple algebraic expressions and apply basic algebraic techniques to solve problems. They extend their use of mathematical vocabulary to talk about numbers and geometrical objects. They begin to understand and follow a short proof, and use geometrical properties to find missing angles and lengths, explaining their reasoning with increasing confidence. They collect data, learn statistical techniques to analyse data and use ICT to present and interpret the results.

Note
This programme of study is intended for those pupils who have not attained a secure level 5 at the end of key stage 3. Teachers are expected to plan work drawing on all the numbered sub-sections of the programme of study.

For some groups of pupils, all or part of particular lettered paragraphs may not be appropriate.

Note about sections
There is no separate section of the programme of study numbered Ma1 that corresponds to the first attainment target, **using and applying mathematics**. Teaching requirements relating to this attainment target are included within the other sections of the programme of study.

1e → links to other subjects
This requirement builds on En1/3b
and En2/1a.

1h, 1i → links to other subjects
These requirements build on En1/1d,
1e and En3/1f, 1i, 1n.

Numbers and the number system

2   Pupils should be taught to:

Integers

a   use their previous understanding of integers and place value to deal with arbitrarily large positive numbers and round them to a given power of 10; understand and use positive numbers, both as positions and translations on a number line; order integers; use the concepts and vocabulary of factor (divisor), multiple and common factor

Powers and roots

b   use the terms square, positive square root, cube; use index notation for squares, cubes and powers of 10; express standard index form both in conventional notation and on a calculator display

Fractions

c   understand equivalent fractions, simplifying a fraction by cancelling all common factors; order fractions by rewriting them with a common denominator

Decimals

d   use decimal notation and recognise that each terminating decimal is a fraction [for example, $0.137 = \frac{137}{1000}$]; order decimals

Percentages

e   understand that 'percentage' means 'number of parts per 100' and use this to compare proportions; interpret percentage as the operator 'so many hundredths of' [for example, 10% means 10 parts per 100 and 15% of Y means $\frac{15}{100} \times Y$]; use percentage in real-life situations [for example, commerce and business, including rate of inflation, VAT and interest rates]

Ratio

f   use ratio notation, including reduction to its simplest form and its various links to fraction notation [for example, in maps and scale drawings, paper sizes and gears].

Calculations

3   Pupils should be taught to:

Number operations and the relationships between them

a   add, subtract, multiply and divide integers and then any number; multiply or divide any number by powers of 10, and any positive number by a number between 0 and 1

b   use brackets and the hierarchy of operations

c   calculate a given fraction of a given quantity [for example, for scale drawings and construction of models, down payments, discounts], expressing the answer as a fraction; express a given number as a fraction of another; add and subtract fractions by writing them with a common denominator; perform short division to convert a simple fraction to a decimal

d   understand and use unit fractions as multiplicative inverses [for example, by thinking of multiplication by $\frac{1}{5}$ as division by 5, or multiplication by $\frac{6}{7}$ as multiplication by 6 followed by division by 7 (or vice versa)]; multiply and divide a fraction by an integer, and multiply a fraction by a unit fraction

e   convert simple fractions of a whole to percentages of the whole and vice versa [for example, analysing diets, budgets or the costs of running, maintaining and owning a car], then understand the multiplicative nature of percentages as operators [for example, 30% increase on £150 gives a total calculated as £(1.3×150) while a 20% discount gives a total calculated as £(0.8×150)]

f   divide a quantity in a given ratio [for example, share £15 in the ratio of 1:2]

Mental methods

g   recall all positive integer complements to 100 [for example, 37 + 63 = 100]; recall all multiplication facts to 10×10, and use them to derive quickly the corresponding division facts; recall the cubes of 2, 3, 4, 5 and 10, and the fraction-to-decimal conversion of familiar simple fractions [for example, $\frac{1}{2}, \frac{1}{4}, \frac{1}{5}, \frac{1}{10}, \frac{1}{100}, \frac{1}{3}, \frac{2}{3}, \frac{1}{8}$]

h   round to the nearest integer and to one significant figure; estimate answers to problems involving decimals

i   develop a range of strategies for mental calculation; derive unknown facts from those they know [for example, estimate $\sqrt{85}$]; add and subtract mentally numbers with up to two decimal places [for example, 13.76 – 5.21, 20.08 + 12.4]; multiply and divide numbers with no more than one decimal digit, [for example, 14.3×4, $56.7 \div 7$] using the commutative, associative, and distributive laws and factorisation where possible, or place value adjustments

Written methods

j   use standard column procedures for addition and subtraction of integers and decimals

k   use standard column procedures for multiplication of integers and decimals, understanding where to position the decimal point by considering what happens if they multiply equivalent fractions; solve a problem involving division by a decimal (up to two places of decimals) by transforming it to a problem involving division by an integer

l   use efficient methods to calculate with fractions, including cancelling common factors before carrying out the calculation, recognising that, in many cases, only a fraction can express the exact answer

Note for 3i
Pupils do not need to know the names of the laws.

45

m   solve simple percentage problems, including increase and decrease [for example, VAT, annual rate of inflation, income tax, discounts]

n   solve word problems about ratio and proportion, including using informal strategies and the unitary method of solution [for example, given that m identical items cost £y, then one item costs £$\frac{y}{m}$ and n items cost £$(n \times \frac{y}{m})$, the number of items that can be bought for £z is $z \times \frac{m}{y}$]

Calculator methods

o   use calculators effectively and efficiently: know how to enter complex calculations and use function keys for reciprocals, squares and powers

p   enter a range of calculations, including those involving standard index form and measures [for example, time calculations in which fractions of an hour must be entered as fractions or as decimals]

q   understand the calculator display, interpreting it correctly [for example, in money calculations, or when the display has been rounded by the calculator], and knowing not to round during the intermediate steps of a calculation.

Solving numerical problems

4   Pupils should be taught to:

a   draw on their knowledge of the operations and the relationships between them, and of simple integer powers and their corresponding roots, to solve problems involving ratio and proportion, a range of measures and compound measures, metric units, and conversion between metric and common imperial units, set in a variety of contexts

b   select appropriate operations, methods and strategies to solve number problems, including trial and improvement where a more efficient method to find the solution is not obvious

c   use a variety of checking procedures, including working the problem backwards, and considering whether a result is of the right order of magnitude

d   give solutions in the context of the problem to an appropriate degree of accuracy, interpreting the solution shown on a calculator display, and recognising limitations on the accuracy of data and measurements.

Equations, formulae and identities

5 Pupils should be taught to:

Use of symbols

a distinguish the different roles played by letter symbols in algebra, knowing that letter symbols represent definite unknown numbers in equations [for example, $5x + 1 = 16$], defined quantities or variables in formulae [for example, $V = IR$], general, unspecified and independent numbers in identities [for example, $3x + 2x = 5x$, $(x + 1)^2 = x^2 + 2x + 1$ for all values of x] and in functions they define new expressions or quantities by referring to known quantities [for example, $y = 2x$]

b understand that the transformation of algebraic expressions obeys and generalises the rules of arithmetic; manipulate algebraic expressions by collecting like terms, by multiplying a single term over a bracket, and by taking out single term common factors [for example, $x + 5 - 2x - 1 = 4 - x$; $5(2x + 3) = 10x + 15$; $x^2 + 3x = x(x + 3)$]; distinguish in meaning between the words 'equation', 'formula', 'identity' and 'expression'

Index notation

c use index notation for simple integer powers, and simple instances of index laws; substitute positive and negative numbers into expressions such as $3x^2 + 4$ and $2x^3$

Inequalities

d solve simple linear inequalities in one variable, and represent the solution set on the number line

Linear equations

e solve linear equations, with integer coefficients, in which the unknown appears on either side or on both sides of the equation; solve linear equations that require prior simplification of brackets, including those that have negative signs occurring anywhere in the equation, and those with a negative solution

Formulae

f use formulae from mathematics and other subjects expressed initially in words and then using letters and symbols [for example, formulae for the area of a triangle, the area enclosed by a circle, wage earned = hours worked × rate per hour]; substitute numbers into a formula; derive a formula and change its subject [for example, convert temperatures between degrees Fahrenheit and degrees Celsius, find the perimeter of a rectangle given its area A and the length l of one side, use $V = IR$ to generate a formula for R in terms of V and I].

5f → ICT opportunity
Pupils could use a spreadsheet to construct formulae to model situations.

6d → ICT opportunity
Pupils could use a spreadsheet to calculate points and draw graphs to explore the effects of varying *m* and *c* in the graph of *y=mx+c*.

Sequences, functions and graphs

6   Pupils should be taught to:

Sequences

a   generate terms of a sequence using term-to-term and position-to-term definitions of the sequence; use linear expressions to describe the nth term of an arithmetic sequence, justifying its form by referring to the activity or context from which it was generated

Graphs of linear functions

b   use the conventions for coordinates in the plane; plot points in all four quadrants; recognise (when values are given for m and c) that equations of the form $y = mx + c$ correspond to straight-line graphs in the coordinate plane; plot graphs of functions in which y is given explicitly in terms of x [for example, $y = 2x + 3$], or implicitly [for example, $x + y = 7$]

c   construct linear functions from real-life problems and plot their corresponding graphs; discuss and interpret graphs arising from real situations; understand that the point of intersection of two different lines in the same two variables that simultaneously describe a real situation is the solution to the simultaneous equations represented by the lines; draw line of best fit through a set of linearly related points and find its equation

Gradients

d   find the gradient of lines given by equations of the form $y = mx + c$ (when values are given for m and c); investigate the gradients of parallel lines

Interpret graphical information

e   interpret information presented in a range of linear and non-linear graphs [for example, graphs describing trends, conversion graphs, distance–time graphs, graphs of height or weight against age, graphs of quantities that vary against time, such as employment].

Ma3 Shape, space and measures

Using and applying shape, space and measures

1   Pupils should be taught to:

Problem solving

a   select problem-solving strategies and resources, including ICT tools,
to use in geometrical work, and monitor their effectiveness

b   select and combine known facts and problem-solving strategies to solve
complex problems

c   identify what further information is needed to solve a geometrical problem;
break complex problems down into a series of tasks

Communicating

d   interpret, discuss and synthesise geometrical information presented in
a variety of forms

e   communicate mathematically, by presenting and organising results and
explaining geometrical diagrams

f   use geometrical language appropriately

g   review and justify their choices of mathematical presentation

Reasoning

h   distinguish between practical demonstrations and proofs

i   apply mathematical reasoning, explaining and justifying inferences and
deductions

j   show step-by-step deduction in solving a geometrical problem

k   state constraints and give starting points when making deductions

l   recognise the limitations of any assumptions that are made; understand
the effects that varying the assumptions may have on the solution

m   identify exceptional cases when solving geometrical problems.

Geometrical reasoning

2   Pupils should be taught to:

Angles

a   recall and use properties of angles at a point, angles on a straight line
(including right angles), perpendicular lines, and opposite angles at a vertex

b   distinguish between acute, obtuse, reflex and right angles; estimate the size
of an angle in degrees

Properties of triangles and other rectilinear shapes

c   use parallel lines, alternate angles and corresponding angles; understand the
properties of parallelograms and a proof that the angle sum of a triangle is
180 degrees; understand a proof that the exterior angle of a triangle is equal
to the sum of the interior angles at the other two vertices

d   use angle properties of equilateral, isosceles and right-angled triangles;
understand congruence; explain why the angle sum of any quadrilateral
is 360 degrees

1d → links to other subjects
This requirement builds on En1/3b
and En2/1a.

1e → links to other subjects
This requirement builds on En1/1d
and En3/1f.

1f → links to other subjects
This requirement builds on En1/1e
and En3/1f.

1g → links to other subjects
This requirement builds on En3/1i, 1n.

e   use their knowledge of rectangles, parallelograms and triangles to deduce formulae for the area of a parallelogram, and a triangle, from the formula for the area of a rectangle

f   recall the essential properties of special types of quadrilateral, including square, rectangle, parallelogram, trapezium and rhombus; classify quadrilaterals by their geometric properties

g   calculate and use the sums of the interior and exterior angles of quadrilaterals, pentagons and hexagons; calculate and use the angles of regular polygons

h   understand, recall and use Pythagoras' theorem

Properties of circles

i   recall the definition of a circle and the meaning of related terms, including centre, radius, chord, diameter, circumference, tangent, arc, sector and segment; understand that inscribed regular polygons can be constructed by equal division of a circle

3-D shapes

j   explore the geometry of cuboids (including cubes), and shapes made from cuboids

k   use 2-D representations of 3-D shapes and analyse 3-D shapes through 2-D projections and cross-sections, including plan and elevation.

Transformations and coordinates

3   Pupils should be taught to:

Specifying transformations

a   understand that rotations are specified by a centre and an (anticlockwise) angle; rotate a shape about the origin, or any other point; measure the angle of rotation using right angles, simple fractions of a turn or degrees; understand that reflections are specified by a mirror line, at first using a line parallel to an axis, then a mirror line such as $y = x$ or $y = -x$; understand that translations are specified by a distance and direction, and enlargements by a centre and positive scale factor

Properties of transformations

b   recognise and visualise rotations, reflections and translations, including reflection symmetry of 2-D and 3-D shapes, and rotation symmetry of 2-D shapes; transform triangles and other 2-D shapes by translation, rotation and reflection, recognising that these transformations preserve length and angle, so that any figure is congruent to its image under any of these transformations

c   recognise, visualise and construct enlargements of objects using positive scale factors greater than one, then positive scale factors less than one; understand from this that any two circles and any two squares are mathematically similar, while, in general, two rectangles are not

d   recognise that enlargements preserve angle but not length; identify the scale factor of an enlargement as the ratio of the lengths of any two corresponding line segments and apply this to triangles; understand the implications of enlargement for perimeter; use and interpret maps and scale drawings; understand the implications of enlargement for area and for volume; distinguish between formulae for perimeter, area and volume by considering dimensions; understand and use simple examples of the relationship between enlargement and areas and volumes of shapes and solids

Coordinates

e   understand that one coordinate identifies a point on a number line, two coordinates identify a point in a plane and three coordinates identify a point in space, using the terms '1-D', '2-D' and '3-D'; use axes and coordinates to specify points in all four quadrants; locate points with given coordinates; find the coordinates of points identified by geometrical information [for example, find the coordinates of the fourth vertex of a parallelogram with vertices at (2, 1) (−7, 3) and (5, 6)]; find the coordinates of the midpoint of the line segment AB, given points A and B, then calculate the length AB.

Measures and construction

4   Pupils should be taught to:

Measures

a   interpret scales on a range of measuring instruments, including those for time and mass; know that measurements using real numbers depend on the choice of unit; recognise that measurements given to the nearest whole unit may be inaccurate by up to one half in either direction; convert measurements from one unit to another; know rough metric equivalents of pounds, feet, miles, pints and gallons; make sensible estimates of a range of measures in everyday settings

b   understand angle measure using the associated language [for example, use bearings to specify direction]

c   understand and use compound measures, including speed

Construction

d   measure and draw lines to the nearest millimetre, and angles to the nearest degree; draw triangles and other 2-D shapes using a ruler and protractor, and given information about their side lengths and angles; understand, from their experience of constructing them, that triangles satisfying SSS, SAS, ASA and RHS are unique, but SSA triangles are not; construct cubes, regular tetrahedra, square-based pyramids and other 3-D shapes from given information e   use straight edge and compasses to do standard constructions, including an equilateral triangle with a given side, the midpoint and perpendicular bisector of a line segment, the perpendicular from a point to a line, the perpendicular from a point on a line, and the bisector of an angle

Mensuration

f   find areas of rectangles, recalling the formula, understanding the connection to counting squares and how it extends this approach; recall and use the formulae for the area of a parallelogram and a triangle; find the surface area of simple shapes using the area formulae for triangles and rectangles; calculate perimeters and areas of shapes made from triangles and rectangles

g   find volumes of cuboids, recalling the formula and understanding the connection to counting cubes and how it extends this approach; calculate volumes of right prisms and of shapes made from cubes and cuboids

h   find circumferences of circles and areas enclosed by circles, recalling relevant formulae

i   convert between area measures, including cm^2 and m^2, and volume measures, including cm^3 and m^3

Loci

j   find loci, both by reasoning and by using ICT to produce shapes and paths [for example, equilateral triangles].

Ma4 Handling data

Using and applying handling data

1   Pupils should be taught to:

Problem solving

a   carry out each of the four aspects of the handling data cycle to solve problems:

   i   specify the problem and plan: formulate questions in terms of the data needed, and consider what inferences can be drawn from the data; decide what data to collect (including sample size and data format) and what statistical analysis is needed

   ii   collect data from a variety of suitable sources, including experiments and surveys, and primary and secondary sources

   iii   process and represent the data: turn the raw data into usable information that gives insight into the problem

   iv   interpret and discuss: answer the initial question by drawing conclusions from the data

b   identify what further information is needed to pursue a particular line of enquiry

c   select and organise the appropriate mathematics and resources to use for a task

d   review progress while working; check and evaluate solutions

Communicating

e   interpret, discuss and synthesise information presented in a variety of forms

f   communicate mathematically, including using ICT, making use of diagrams and related explanatory text

g   examine critically, and justify, their choices of mathematical presentation of problems involving data

Reasoning

h   apply mathematical reasoning, explaining and justifying inferences and deductions

i   explore connections in mathematics and look for cause and effect when analysing data

j   recognise the limitations of any assumptions and the effects that varying the assumptions could have on conclusions drawn from the data analysis.

1e → links to other subjects
This requirement builds on En1/3b and En2/1a.

1f → links to other subjects
This requirement builds on En1/1d and En3/1f.

1g → links to other subjects
This requirement builds on En1/1e, 3b and En3/1i, 1n.

Specifying the problem and planning

2   Pupils should be taught to:

   a   see that random processes are unpredictable

   b   identify questions that can be addressed by statistical methods

   c   discuss how data relate to a problem; identify possible sources of bias and plan to minimise it

   d   identify which primary data they need to collect and in what format, including grouped data, considering appropriate equal class intervals

   e   design an experiment or survey; decide what secondary data to use.

Collecting data

3   Pupils should be taught to:

   a   design and use data-collection sheets for grouped discrete and continuous data; collect data using various methods, including observation, controlled experiment, data logging, questionnaires and surveys

   b   gather data from secondary sources, including printed tables and lists from ICT-based sources

   c   design and use two-way tables for discrete and grouped data.

Processing and representing data

4   Pupils should be taught to:

   a   draw and produce, using paper and ICT, pie charts for categorical data, and diagrams for continuous data, including line graphs for time series, scatter graphs, frequency diagrams and stem-and-leaf diagrams

   b   calculate mean, range and median of small data sets with discrete then continuous data; identify the modal class for grouped data

   c   understand and use the probability scale

   d   understand and use estimates or measures of probability from theoretical models (including equally likely outcomes), or from relative frequency

   e   list all outcomes for single events, and for two successive events, in a systematic way

   f   identify different mutually exclusive outcomes and know that the sum of the probabilities of all these outcomes is 1

   g   find the median for large data sets and calculate an estimate of the mean for large data sets with grouped data

   h   draw lines of best fit by eye, understanding what these represent.

Interpreting and discussing results

5   Pupils should be taught to:

a   relate summarised data to the initial questions

b   interpret a wide range of graphs and diagrams and draw conclusions

c   look at data to find patterns and exceptions

d   compare distributions and make inferences, using the shapes of distributions and measures of average and range

e   consider and check results and modify their approach if necessary

f   have a basic understanding of correlation as a measure of the strength of the association between two variables; identify correlation or no correlation using lines of best fit

g   use the vocabulary of probability to interpret results involving uncertainty and prediction

h   compare experimental data and theoretical probabilities

i   understand that if they repeat an experiment, they may – and usually will – get different outcomes, and that increasing sample size generally leads to better estimates of probability and population characteristics

j   discuss implications of findings in the context of the problem

k   interpret social statistics including index numbers [for example, the General Index of Retail Prices]; time series [for example, population growth]; and survey data [for example, the National Census].

5c → **ICT opportunity**
Pupils could use databases to present their findings.

Breadth of study

1 During the key stage, pupils should be taught the **Knowledge, skills and understanding** through:

a extending mental and written calculation strategies and using efficient procedures confidently to calculate with integers, fractions, decimals, percentages, ratio and proportion

b solving a range of familiar and unfamiliar problems, including those drawn from real-life contexts and other areas of the curriculum

c activities that provide frequent opportunities to discuss their work, to develop reasoning and understanding and to explain their reasoning and strategies

d activities focused on developing short chains of deductive reasoning and correct use of the '=' sign

e activities in which they do practical work with geometrical objects, visualise them and work with them mentally

f practical work in which they draw inferences from data, consider how statistics are used in real life to make informed decisions, and recognise the difference between meaningful and misleading representations of data

g activities focused on the major ideas of statistics, including using appropriate populations and representative samples, using different measurement scales, using probability as a measure of uncertainty, using randomness and variability, reducing bias in sampling and measuring, and using inference to make decisions

h substantial use of tasks focused on using appropriate ICT [for example, spreadsheets, databases, geometry or graphic packages], using calculators correctly and efficiently, and knowing when not to use a calculator.

Programme of study: mathematics higher

Key stage 4

Knowledge, skills and understanding

Teaching should ensure that appropriate connections are made between the sections on **number and algebra**, **shape, space and measures**, and **handling data**.

Ma2 Number and algebra

Using and applying number and algebra

1 Pupils should be taught to:

Problem solving

a select and use appropriate and efficient techniques and strategies to solve problems of increasing complexity, involving numerical and algebraic manipulation

b identify what further information may be required in order to pursue a particular line of enquiry and give reasons for following or rejecting particular approaches

c break down a complex calculation into simpler steps before attempting a solution and justify their choice of methods

d make mental estimates of the answers to calculations; present answers to sensible levels of accuracy; understand how errors are compounded in certain calculations

Communicating

e discuss their work and explain their reasoning using an increasing range of mathematical language and notation

f use a variety of strategies and diagrams for establishing algebraic or graphical representations of a problem and its solution; move from one form of representation to another to get different perspectives on the problem

g present and interpret solutions in the context of the original problem

h use notation and symbols correctly and consistently within a given problem

i examine critically, improve, then justify their choice of mathematical presentation; present a concise, reasoned argument

Reasoning

j explore, identify, and use pattern and symmetry in algebraic contexts, investigating whether a particular case may be generalised further and understand the importance of a counter-example; identify exceptional cases when solving problems

k understand the difference between a practical demonstration and a proof

l show step-by-step deduction in solving a problem; derive proofs using short chains of deductive reasoning

During key stage 4 (higher) pupils take increasing responsibility for planning and executing their work. They refine their calculating skills to include powers, roots and numbers expressed in standard form. They learn the importance of precision and rigour in mathematics. They use proportional reasoning with fluency and develop skills of algebraic manipulation and simplification. They extend their knowledge of functions and related graphs and solve a range of equations, including those with non-integer coefficients. They use short chains of deductive reasoning, develop their own proofs, and begin to understand the importance of proof in mathematics. Pupils use definitions and formal reasoning to describe and understand geometrical figures and the logical relationships between them. They learn to handle data through practical activities, using a broader range of skills and techniques, including sampling. Pupils develop the confidence and flexibility to solve unfamiliar problems and to use ICT appropriately. By seeing the importance of mathematics as an analytical tool for solving problems, they learn to appreciate its unique power.

Note

This programme of study is intended for pupils who have attained a secure level 5 at the end of key stage 3. Teachers are expected to plan work drawing on all the numbered sub-sections of the programme of study.

For some groups of pupils, all or part of particular lettered paragraphs may not be appropriate.

Note about sections

There is no separate section of the programme of study numbered Ma1 that corresponds to the first attainment target, **using and applying mathematics**. Teaching requirements relating to this attainment target are included within the other sections of the programme of study.

1e → links to other subjects
This requirement builds on En1/1d, 1e.

1f → links to other subjects
This requirement builds on En1/1d.

1g → links to other subjects
This requirement builds on En3/1f, 1n.

1i → links to other subjects
This requirement builds on En1/1e,
3b and En2/1a and En3/1f, 1i.

m   recognise the significance of stating constraints and assumptions when deducing results; recognise the limitations of any assumptions that are made and the effect that varying the assumptions may have on the solution to a problem.

Numbers and the number system

2   Pupils should be taught to:

Integers

a   use their previous understanding of integers and place value to deal with arbitrarily large positive numbers and round them to a given power of 10; understand and use negative integers both as positions and translations on a number line; order integers; use the concepts and vocabulary of factor (divisor), multiple, common factor, highest common factor, least common multiple, prime number and prime factor decomposition

Powers and roots

b   use the terms square, positive square root, negative square root, cube and cube root; use index notation [for example, 8^2, $8^{\frac{1}{3}}$] and index laws for multiplication and division of integer powers; use standard index form, expressed in conventional notation and on a calculator display

Fractions

c   understand equivalent fractions, simplifying a fraction by cancelling all common factors; order fractions by rewriting them with a common denominator

Decimals

d   recognise that each terminating decimal is a fraction [for example, $0.137 = \frac{137}{1000}$]; recognise that recurring decimals are exact fractions, and that some exact fractions are recurring decimals [for example, $\frac{1}{7} = 0.142857142857...$]; order decimals

Percentages

e   understand that 'percentage' means 'number of parts per 100', and interpret percentage as the operator 'so many hundredths of' [for example, 10% means 10 parts per 100 and 15% of Y means $\frac{15}{100} \times Y$]

Ratio

f   use ratio notation, including reduction to its simplest form and its various links to fraction notation.

Calculations

3   Pupils should be taught to:

Number operations and the relationships between them

a   multiply or divide any number by powers of 10, and any positive number
by a number between 0 and 1; find the prime factor decomposition of
positive integers; understand 'reciprocal' as multiplicative inverse, knowing
that any non-zero number multiplied by its reciprocal is 1 (and that zero has
no reciprocal, because division by zero is not defined); multiply and divide
by a negative number; use index laws to simplify and calculate the value of
numerical expressions involving multiplication and division of integer,
fractional and negative powers; use inverse operations, understanding that
the inverse operation of raising a positive number to power n is raising the
result of this operation to power $\frac{1}{n}$

b   use brackets and the hierarchy of operations

c   calculate a given fraction of a given quantity, expressing the answer as a
fraction; express a given number as a fraction of another; add and subtract
fractions by writing them with a common denominator; perform short
division to convert a simple fraction to a decimal; distinguish between
fractions with denominators that have only prime factors of 2 and 5 (which
are represented by terminating decimals), and other fractions (which are
represented by recurring decimals); convert a recurring decimal to a fraction
[for example, $0.142857142857\ldots = \frac{1}{7}$]

d   understand and use unit fractions as multiplicative inverses [for example,
by thinking of multiplication by $\frac{1}{5}$ as division by 5, or multiplication by $\frac{6}{7}$ as
multiplication by 6 followed by division by 7 (or vice versa)]; multiply and
divide a given fraction by an integer, by a unit fraction and by a general
fraction

e   convert simple fractions of a whole to percentages of the whole and vice
versa; then understand the multiplicative nature of percentages as operators
[for example, a 15% increase in value Y, followed by a 15% decrease is
calculated as $1.15 \times 0.85 \times Y$]; calculate an original amount when given the
transformed amount after a percentage change; reverse percentage problems
[for example, given that a meal in a restaurant costs £36 with VAT at 17.5%,
its price before VAT is calculated as $£\frac{36}{1.175}$]

f   divide a quantity in a given ratio

Note for 3n

Numbers that can be written as the ratio of two integers are known as rational numbers. Surds and π are examples of irrational numbers, which cannot be written as the ratio of two integers.

Mental methods

g   recall integer squares from 2×2 to 15×15 and the corresponding square roots, the cubes of 2, 3, 4, 5 and 10, the fact that $n^0 = 1$ and $n^{-1} = \frac{1}{n}$ for positive integers n [for example, $10^0 = 1$; $9^{-1} = \frac{1}{9}$], the corresponding rule for negative numbers [for example, $5^{-2} = \frac{1}{5^2} = \frac{1}{25}$], $n^{\frac{1}{2}} = \sqrt{n}$ and $n^{\frac{1}{3}} = \sqrt[3]{n}$ for any positive number n [for example, $25^{\frac{1}{2}} = 5$ and $64^{\frac{1}{3}} = 4$]

h   round to a given number of significant figures; develop a range of strategies for mental calculation; derive unknown facts from those they know; convert between ordinary and standard index form representations [for example, $0.1234 = 1.234 \times 10^{-1}$], converting to standard index form to make sensible estimates for calculations involving multiplication and/or division

Written methods

i   use efficient methods to calculate with fractions, including cancelling common factors before carrying out the calculation, recognising that in many cases only a fraction can express the exact answer

j   solve percentage problems, including percentage increase and decrease [for example, simple interest, VAT, annual rate of inflation]; and reverse percentages

k   represent repeated proportional change using a multiplier raised to a power [for example, compound interest]

l   calculate an unknown quantity from quantities that vary in direct or inverse proportion

m   calculate with standard index form [for example, $2.4 \times 10^7 \times 5 \times 10^3 = 12 \times 10^{10} = 1.2 \times 10^{11}$, $(2.4 \times 10^7) \div (5 \times 10^3) = 4.8 \times 10^3$]

n   use surds and π in exact calculations, without a calculator; rationalise a denominator such as $\frac{1}{\sqrt{3}} = \frac{\sqrt{3}}{3}$

Calculator methods

o   use calculators effectively and efficiently, knowing how to enter complex calculations; use an extended range of function keys, including trigonometrical and statistical functions relevant across this programme of study

p   understand the calculator display, knowing when to interpret the display, when the display has been rounded by the calculator, and not to round during the intermediate steps of a calculation

q   use calculators, or written methods, to calculate the upper and lower bounds of calculations, particularly when working with measurements

r   use standard index form display and how to enter numbers in standard index form

s   use calculators for reverse percentage calculations by doing an appropriate division

t   use calculators to explore exponential growth and decay [for example, in science or geography], using a multiplier and the power key.

Solving numerical problems

4   Pupils should be taught to:

a   draw on their knowledge of operations and inverse operations (including powers and roots), and of methods of simplification (including factorisation and the use of the commutative, associative and distributive laws of addition, multiplication and factorisation) in order to select and use suitable strategies and techniques to solve problems and word problems, including those involving ratio and proportion, repeated proportional change, fractions, percentages and reverse percentages, inverse proportion, surds, measures and conversion between measures, and compound measures defined within a particular situation

b   check and estimate answers to problems; select and justify appropriate degrees of accuracy for answers to problems; recognise limitations on the accuracy of data and measurements.

Equations, formulae and identities

5   Pupils should be taught to:

Use of symbols

a   distinguish the different roles played by letter symbols in algebra, using the correct notational conventions for multiplying or dividing by a given number, and knowing that letter symbols represent definite unknown numbers in equations [for example, $x^2 + 1 = 82$], defined quantities or variables in formula [for example, $V = IR$], general, unspecified and independent numbers in identities [for example, $(x + 1)^2 = x^2 + 2x + 1$ for all x], and in functions they define new expressions or quantities by referring to known quantities [for example, $y = 2 - 7x$; $f(x) = x^3$; $y = \frac{1}{x}$ with $x \neq 0$]

b   understand that the transformation of algebraic entities obeys and generalises the well-defined rules of generalised arithmetic [for example, $a(b + c) = ab + ac$]; expand the product of two linear expressions [for example, $(x + 1)(x + 2) = x^2 + 3x + 2$]; manipulate algebraic expressions by collecting like terms, multiplying a single term over a bracket, taking out common factors [for example, $9x - 3 = 3(3x - 1)$], factorising quadratic expressions including the difference of two squares [for example, $x^2 - 9 = (x + 3)(x - 3)$] and cancelling common factors in rational expressions [for example, $2(x + 1)^2/(x + 1) = 2(x + 1)$]

c   know the meaning of and use the words 'equation', 'formula', 'identity' and 'expression'

Index notation

d   use index notation for simple integer powers, and simple instances of index laws [for example, $x^3 \times x^2 = x^5$; $\frac{x^2}{x^3} = x^{-1}$; $(x^2)^3 = x^6$]; substitute positive and negative numbers into expressions such as $3x^2 + 4$ and $2x^3$

5g → ICT opportunity
Pupils could use a spreadsheet or graphic calculator to construct and use formulae.

Equations

e   set up simple equations [for example, find the angle a in a triangle with angles a, $a + 10$, $a + 20$]; solve simple equations [for example, $5x = 7$; $11 - 4x = 2$; $3(2x + 1) = 8$; $2(1 - x) = 6(2 + x)$; $4x^2 = 49$; $3 = \frac{12}{x}$] by using inverse operations or by transforming both sides in the same way

Linear equations

f   solve linear equations in one unknown, with integer or fractional coefficients, in which the unknown appears on either side or on both sides of the equation; solve linear equations that require prior simplification of brackets, including those that have negative signs occurring anywhere in the equation, and those with a negative solution

Formulae

g   use formulae from mathematics and other subjects [for example, for area of a triangle or a parallelogram, area enclosed by a circle, volume of a prism, volume of a cone]; substitute numbers into a formula; change the subject of a formula, including cases where the subject occurs twice, or where a power of the subject appears [for example, find r given that $A = \pi r^2$, find x given $y = mx + c$]; generate a formula [for example, find the perimeter of a rectangle given its area A and the length l of one side]

Direct and inverse proportion

h   set up and use equations to solve word and other problems involving direct proportion or inverse proportion [for example, $y \propto x$, $y \propto x^2$, $y \propto \frac{1}{x}$, $y \propto \frac{1}{x^2}$] and relate algebraic solutions to graphical representation of the equations

Simultaneous linear equations

i   find the exact solution of two simultaneous equations in two unknowns by eliminating a variable, and interpret the equations as lines and their common solution as the point of intersection

j   solve simple linear inequalities in one variable, and represent the solution set on a number line; solve several linear inequalities in two variables and find the solution set

Quadratic equations

k   solve quadratic equations by factorisation, completing the square and using the quadratic formula

Simultaneous linear and quadratic equations

l   solve exactly, by elimination of an unknown, two simultaneous equations in two unknowns, one of which is linear in each unknown, and the other is linear in one unknown and quadratic in the other [for example, solve the simultaneous equations $y = 11x - 2$ and $y = 5x^2$], or where the second is of the form $x^2 + y^2 = r^2$

Numerical methods

m   use systematic trial and improvement to find approximate solutions
    of equations where there is no simple analytical method of solving
    them [for example, $x^3 - x = 900$].

Sequences, functions and graphs

6   Pupils should be taught to:

Sequences

a   generate common integer sequences (including sequences of odd or even
    integers, squared integers, powers of 2, powers of 10, triangular numbers);
    generate terms of a sequence using term-to-term and position-to-term
    definitions of the sequence; use linear expressions to describe the nth term
    of an arithmetic sequence, justifying its form by reference to the activity
    or context from which it was generated

Graphs of linear functions

b   use conventions for coordinates in the plane; plot points in all four
    quadrants; recognise (when values are given for m and c) that equations
    of the form $y = mx + c$ correspond to straight-line graphs in the coordinate
    plane; plot graphs of functions in which y is given explicitly in terms of
    x (as in $y = 2x + 3$), or implicitly (as in $x + y = 7$)

c   find the gradient of lines given by equations of the form $y = mx + c$ (when
    values are given for m and c); understand that the form $y = mx + c$ represents
    a straight line and that m is the gradient of the line, and c is the value of the
    y-intercept; explore the gradients of parallel lines and lines perpendicular to
    these lines [for example, know that the lines represented by the equations
    $y = -5x$ and $y = 3 - 5x$ are parallel, each having gradient (-5) and that the
    line with equation $y = \frac{x}{5}$ is perpendicular to these lines and has gradient $\frac{1}{5}$]

Interpreting graphical information

d   construct linear functions and plot the corresponding graphs arising from
    real-life problems; discuss and interpret graphs modelling real situations
    [for example, distance–time graph for a particle moving with constant
    speed, the depth of water in a container as it empties, the velocity–time
    graph for a particle moving with constant acceleration]

Quadratic functions

e   generate points and plot graphs of simple quadratic functions [for example,
    $y = x^2$; $y = 3x^2 + 4$], then more general quadratic functions [for example,
    $y = x^2 - 2x + 1$]; find approximate solutions of a quadratic equation from the
    graph of the corresponding quadratic function; find the intersection points
    of the graphs of a linear and quadratic function, knowing that these are the
    approximate solutions of the corresponding simultaneous equations
    representing the linear and quadratic functions

6b–6f → **ICT opportunity**
Pupils could generate functions from plots of
data, for example, from a science experiment,
using simple curve fitting techniques on
graphic calculators, or with graphics software.

6g → ICT opportunity
Pupils could use software to explore transformations of graphs.

Note for 6h
The derivation of the circle equation is an application of Pythagoras' theorem. Loci can be considered from an algebraic point of view as here or from a geometric point of view as in Ma3/3e.

Other functions

f   plot graphs of: simple cubic functions [for example, $y = x^3$], the reciprocal function $y = \frac{1}{x}$ with $x \neq 0$, the exponential function $y = k^x$ for integer values of x and simple positive values of k [for example, $y = 2^x$; $y = (\frac{1}{2})^x$], the circular functions $y = \sin x$ and $y = \cos x$, using a spreadsheet or graph plotter as well as pencil and paper; recognise the characteristic shapes of all these functions

Transformation of functions

g   apply to the graph of $y = f(x)$ the transformations $y = f(x) + a$, $y = f(ax)$, $y = f(x + a)$, $y = af(x)$ for linear, quadratic, sine and cosine functions $f(x)$

Loci

h   construct the graphs of simple loci, including the circle $x^2 + y^2 = r^2$ for a circle of radius r centred at the origin of coordinates; find graphically the intersection points of a given straight line with this circle and know that this corresponds to solving the two simultaneous equations representing the line and the circle.

Ma3 Shape, space and measures

Using and applying shape, space and measures

1   Pupils should be taught to:

Problem-solving

a   select the problem-solving strategies to use in geometrical work, and consider and explain the extent to which the selections they made were appropriate

b   select and combine known facts and problem-solving strategies to solve more complex geometrical problems

c   develop and follow alternative lines of enquiry, justifying their decisions to follow or reject particular approaches

Communicating

d   communicate mathematically, with emphasis on a critical examination of the presentation and organisation of results, and on effective use of symbols and geometrical diagrams

e   use precise formal language and exact methods for analysing geometrical configurations

Reasoning

f   apply mathematical reasoning, progressing from brief mathematical explanations towards full justifications in more complex contexts

g   explore connections in geometry; pose conditional constraints of the type 'If … then …'; and ask questions 'What if …?' or 'Why?'

h   show step-by-step deduction in solving a geometrical problem

i   state constraints and give starting points when making deductions

j   understand the necessary and sufficient conditions under which generalisations, inferences and solutions to geometrical problems remain valid.

Geometrical reasoning

2   Pupils should be taught to:

Properties of triangles and other rectilinear shapes

a   distinguish between lines and line segments; use parallel lines, alternate angles and corresponding angles; understand the consequent properties of parallelograms and a proof that the angle sum of a triangle is 180 degrees; understand a proof that the exterior angle of a triangle is equal to the sum of the interior angles at the other two vertices

b   use angle properties of equilateral, isosceles and right-angled triangles; explain why the angle sum of a quadrilateral is 360 degrees

1d, 1e → links to other subjects
These requirements build on En1/1d, 1e and En3/1f, 1i, 1n.

c   recall the definitions of special types of quadrilateral, including square, rectangle, parallelogram, trapezium and rhombus; classify quadrilaterals by their geometric properties

d   calculate and use the sums of the interior and exterior angles of quadrilaterals, pentagons, hexagons; calculate and use the angles of regular polygons

e   understand and use SSS, SAS, ASA and RHS conditions to prove the congruence of triangles using formal arguments, and to verify standard ruler and compass constructions

f   understand, recall and use Pythagoras' theorem in 2-D, then 3-D problems; investigate the geometry of cuboids including cubes, and shapes made from cuboids, including the use of Pythagoras' theorem to calculate lengths in three dimensions

g   understand similarity of triangles and of other plane figures, and use this to make geometric inferences; understand, recall and use trigonometrical relationships in right-angled triangles, and use these to solve problems, including those involving bearings, then use these relationships in 3-D contexts, including finding the angles between a line and a plane (but not the angle between two planes or between two skew lines); calculate the area of a triangle using $\frac{1}{2}ab \sin C$; draw, sketch and describe the graphs of trigonometric functions for angles of any size, including transformations involving scalings in either or both the x and y directions; use the sine and cosine rules to solve 2-D and 3-D problems

Properties of circles

h   recall the definition of a circle and the meaning of related terms, including centre, radius, chord, diameter, circumference, tangent, arc, sector and segment; understand that the tangent at any point on a circle is perpendicular to the radius at that point; understand and use the fact that tangents from an external point are equal in length; explain why the perpendicular from the centre to a chord bisects the chord; understand that inscribed regular polygons can be constructed by equal division of a circle; prove and use the facts that the angle subtended by an arc at the centre of a circle is twice the angle subtended at any point on the circumference, the angle subtended at the circumference by a semicircle is a right angle, that angles in the same segment are equal, and that opposite angles of a cyclic quadrilateral sum to 180 degrees; prove and use the alternate segment theorem

i   use 2-D representations of 3-D shapes and analyse 3-D shapes through 2-D projections and cross-sections, including plan and elevation; solve problems involving surface areas and volumes of prisms, pyramids, cylinders, cones and spheres; solve problems involving more complex shapes and solids, including segments of circles and frustums of cones.

Transformations and coordinates

3   Pupils should be taught to:

Specifying transformations

a   understand that rotations are specified by a centre and an (anticlockwise) angle; use any point as the centre of rotation; measure the angle of rotation, using right angles, fractions of a turn or degrees; understand that reflections are specified by a (mirror) line; understand that translations are specified by giving a distance and direction (or a vector), and enlargements by a centre and a positive scale factor

Properties of transformations

b   recognise and visualise rotations, reflections and translations including reflection symmetry of 2-D and 3-D shapes, and rotation symmetry of 2-D shapes; transform triangles and other 2-D shapes by translation, rotation and reflection and combinations of these transformations; use congruence to show that translations, rotations and reflections preserve length and angle, so that any figure is congruent to its image under any of these transformations; distinguish properties that are preserved under particular transformations

c   recognise, visualise and construct enlargements of objects; understand from this that any two circles and any two squares are mathematically similar, while, in general, two rectangles are not, then use positive fractional and negative scale factors

d   recognise that enlargements preserve angle but not length; identify the scale factor of an enlargement as the ratio of the lengths of any two corresponding line segments; understand the implications of enlargement for perimeter; use and interpret maps and scale drawings; understand the difference between formulae for perimeter, area and volume by considering dimensions; understand and use the effect of enlargement on areas and volumes of shapes and solids

Coordinates

e   understand that one coordinate identifies a point on a number line, that two coordinates identify a point in a plane and three coordinates identify a point in space, using the terms '1-D', '2-D' and '3-D'; use axes and coordinates to specify points in all four quadrants; locate points with given coordinates; find the coordinates of points identified by geometrical information; find the coordinates of the midpoint of the line segment AB, given the points A and B, then calculate the length AB

3b–3f → ICT opportunity
Pupils could use software to explore transformations and their effects on properties of shapes.

Vectors

f understand and use vector notation; calculate, and represent graphically the sum of two vectors, the difference of two vectors and a scalar multiple of a vector; calculate the resultant of two vectors; understand and use the commutative and associative properties of vector addition; solve simple geometrical problems in 2-D using vector methods.

Measures and construction

4 Pupils should be taught to:

Measures

a use angle measure [for example, use bearings to specify direction]; know that measurements using real numbers depend on the choice of unit; recognise that measurements given to the nearest whole unit may be inaccurate by up to one half in either direction; convert measurements from one unit to another; understand and use compound measures, including speed and density

Construction

b draw approximate constructions of triangles and other 2-D shapes, using a ruler and protractor, given information about side lengths and angles; construct specified cubes, regular tetrahedra, square-based pyramids and other 3-D shapes

c use straight edge and compasses to do standard constructions including an equilateral triangle with a given side, the midpoint and perpendicular bisector of a line segment, the perpendicular from a point to a line, the perpendicular from a point on a line, and the bisector of an angle

Mensuration

d find the surface area of simple shapes by using the formulae for the areas of triangles and rectangles; find volumes of cuboids, recalling the formula and understanding the connection to counting cubes and how it extends this approach; calculate volumes of right prisms and of shapes made from cubes and cuboids; convert between volume measures including cm^3 and m^3; find circumferences of circles and areas enclosed by circles, recalling relevant formulae; calculate the lengths of arcs and the areas of sectors of circles

Loci

e find loci, both by reasoning and by using ICT to produce shapes and paths [for example, a region bounded by a circle and an intersecting line].

Ma4 Handling data

Using and applying handling data

1   Pupils should be taught to:

Problem solving

a   carry out each of the four aspects of the handling data cycle to solve problems:

   i   specify the problem and plan: formulate questions in terms of the data needed, and consider what inferences can be drawn from the data; decide what data to collect (including sample size and data format) and what statistical analysis is needed)

   ii   collect data from a variety of suitable sources, including experiments and surveys, and primary and secondary sources

   iii   process and represent the data: turn the raw data into usable information that gives insight into the problem

   iv   interpret and discuss the data: answer the initial question by drawing conclusions from the data

b   select the problem-solving strategies to use in statistical work, and monitor their effectiveness (these strategies should address the scale and manageability of the tasks, and should consider whether the mathematics and approach used are delivering the most appropriate solutions)

Communicating

c   communicate mathematically, with emphasis on the use of an increasing range of diagrams and related explanatory text, on the selection of their mathematical presentation, explaining its purpose and approach, and on the use of symbols to convey statistical meaning

Reasoning

d   apply mathematical reasoning, explaining and justifying inferences and deductions, justifying arguments and solutions

e   identify exceptional or unexpected cases when solving statistical problems

f   explore connections in mathematics and look for relationships between variables when analysing data

g   recognise the limitations of any assumptions and the effects that varying the assumptions could have on the conclusions drawn from data analysis.

Specifying the problem and planning

2   Pupils should be taught to:

a   see that random processes are unpredictable

b   identify key questions that can be addressed by statistical methods

c   discuss how data relate to a problem; identify possible sources of bias and plan to minimise it

1c → links to other subjects
This requirement builds on En1/1d, 1e and En3/1f, 1i, 1n.

1c → ICT opportunity
Pupils could use databases or spreadsheets to present their findings and display their data.

d   identify which primary data they need to collect and in what format, including grouped data, considering appropriate equal class intervals; select and justify a sampling scheme and a method to investigate a population, including random and stratified sampling

e   design an experiment or survey; decide what primary and secondary data to use.

Collecting data

3   Pupils should be taught to:

a   collect data using various methods, including observation, controlled experiment, data logging, questionnaires and surveys

b   gather data from secondary sources, including printed tables and lists from ICT-based sources

c   design and use two-way tables for discrete and grouped data

d   deal with practical problems such as non-response or missing data.

Processing and representing data

4   Pupils should be taught to:

a   draw and produce, using paper and ICT, pie charts for categorical data, and diagrams for continuous data, including line graphs (time series), scatter graphs, frequency diagrams, stem-and-leaf diagrams, cumulative frequency tables and diagrams, box plots and histograms for grouped continuous data

b   understand and use estimates or measures of probability from theoretical models, or from relative frequency

c   list all outcomes for single events, and for two successive events, in a systematic way

d   identify different mutually exclusive outcomes and know that the sum of the probabilities of all these outcomes is 1

e   find the median, quartiles and interquartile range for large data sets and calculate the mean for large data sets with grouped data

f   calculate an appropriate moving average

g   know when to add or multiply two probabilities: if A and B are mutually exclusive, then the probability of A or B occurring is $P(A) + P(B)$, whereas if A and B are independent events, the probability of A and B occurring is $P(A) \times P(B)$

h   use tree diagrams to represent outcomes of compound events, recognising when events are independent

i   draw lines of best fit by eye, understanding what these represent

j   use relevant statistical functions on a calculator or spreadsheet.

Interpreting and discussing results

5 Pupils should be taught to:

a relate summarised data to the initial questions

b interpret a wide range of graphs and diagrams and draw conclusions; identify seasonality and trends in time series

c look at data to find patterns and exceptions

d compare distributions and make inferences, using shapes of distributions and measures of average and spread, including median and quartiles; understand frequency density

e consider and check results, and modify their approaches if necessary

f appreciate that correlation is a measure of the strength of the association between two variables; distinguish between positive, negative and zero correlation using lines of best fit; appreciate that zero correlation does not necessarily imply 'no relationship' but merely 'no linear relationship'

g use the vocabulary of probability to interpret results involving uncertainty and prediction [for example, 'there is some evidence from this sample that …']

h compare experimental data and theoretical probabilities

i understand that if they repeat an experiment, they may – and usually will – get different outcomes, and that increasing sample size generally leads to better estimates of probability and population parameters.

5c → ICT opportunity
Pupils could use databases to present their findings.

Breadth of study

1   During the key stage, pupils should be taught the **Knowledge, skills and understanding** through:

   a   activities that ensure they become familiar with and confident using standard procedures for the range of calculations appropriate to this level of study

   b   solving familiar and unfamiliar problems in a range of numerical, algebraic and graphical contexts and in open-ended and closed form

   c   using standard notations for decimals, fractions, percentages, ratio and indices

   d   activities that show how algebra, as an extension of number using symbols, gives precise form to mathematical relationships and calculations

   e   activities in which they progress from using definitions and short chains of reasoning to understanding and formulating proofs in algebra and geometry

   f   a sequence of practical activities that address increasingly demanding statistical problems in which they draw inferences from data and consider the uses of statistics in society

   g   choosing appropriate ICT tools and using these to solve numerical and graphical problems, to represent and manipulate geometrical configurations and to present and analyse data.

General teaching requirements

Inclusion: providing effective learning opportunities for all pupils

Schools have a responsibility to provide a broad and balanced curriculum for all pupils. The National Curriculum is the starting point for planning a school curriculum that meets the specific needs of individuals and groups of pupils. This statutory inclusion statement on providing effective learning opportunities for all pupils outlines how teachers can modify, as necessary, the National Curriculum programmes of study to provide all pupils with relevant and appropriately challenging work at each key stage. It sets out three principles that are essential to developing a more inclusive curriculum:

A Setting suitable learning challenges

B Responding to pupils' diverse learning needs

C Overcoming potential barriers to learning and assessment for individuals and groups of pupils.

Applying these principles should keep to a minimum the need for aspects of the National Curriculum to be disapplied for a pupil.

Schools are able to provide other curricular opportunities outside the National Curriculum to meet the needs of individuals or groups of pupils such as speech and language therapy and mobility training.

Three principles for inclusion

In planning and teaching the National Curriculum, teachers are required to have due regard to the following principles.

A Setting suitable learning challenges

1 Teachers should aim to give every pupil the opportunity to experience success in learning and to achieve as high a standard as possible. The National Curriculum programmes of study set out what most pupils should be taught at each key stage – but teachers should teach the knowledge, skills and understanding in ways that suit their pupils' abilities. This may mean choosing knowledge, skills and understanding from earlier or later key stages so that individual pupils can make progress and show what they can achieve. Where it is appropriate for pupils to make extensive use of content from an earlier key stage, there may not be time to teach all aspects of the age-related programmes of study. A similarly flexible approach will be needed to take account of any gaps in pupils' learning resulting from missed or interrupted schooling [for example, that may be experienced by travellers, refugees, those in care or those with long-term medical conditions, including pupils with neurological problems, such as head injuries, and those with degenerative conditions].

2   For pupils whose attainments fall significantly below the expected levels at a particular key stage, a much greater degree of differentiation will be necessary. In these circumstances, teachers may need to use the content of the programmes of study as a resource or to provide a context, in planning learning appropriate to the age and requirements of their pupils.[1]

3   For pupils whose attainments significantly exceed the expected level of attainment within one or more subjects during a particular key stage, teachers will need to plan suitably challenging work. As well as drawing on materials from later key stages or higher levels of study, teachers may plan further differentiation by extending the breadth and depth of study within individual subjects or by planning work which draws on the content of different subjects.[2]

B   Responding to pupils' diverse learning needs

1   When planning, teachers should set high expectations and provide opportunities for all pupils to achieve, including boys and girls, pupils with special educational needs, pupils with disabilities, pupils from all social and cultural backgrounds, pupils of different ethnic groups including travellers, refugees and asylum seekers, and those from diverse linguistic backgrounds. Teachers need to be aware that pupils bring to school different experiences, interests and strengths which will influence the way in which they learn. Teachers should plan their approaches to teaching and learning so that all pupils can take part in lessons fully and effectively.

2   To ensure that they meet the full range of pupils' needs, teachers should be aware of the requirements of the equal opportunities legislation that covers race, gender and disability.[3]

3   Teachers should take specific action to respond to pupils' diverse needs by:
    a   creating effective learning environments
    b   securing their motivation and concentration
    c   providing equality of opportunity through teaching approaches
    d   using appropriate assessment approaches
    e   setting targets for learning.

Examples for B/3a – creating effective learning environments
Teachers create effective learning environments in which:
- the contribution of all pupils is valued
- all pupils can feel secure and are able to contribute appropriately
- stereotypical views are challenged and pupils learn to appreciate and view positively differences in others, whether arising from race, gender, ability or disability

---

[1] Teachers may find QCA's guidance on planning work for pupils with learning difficulties a helpful companion to the programmes of study.
[2] Teachers may find QCA's guidance on meeting the requirements of gifted and talented pupils a helpful companion to the programmes of study.
[3] The Sex Discrimination Act 1975, the Race Relations Act 1976, the Disability Discrimination Act 1995.

- pupils learn to take responsibility for their actions and behaviours both in school and in the wider community
- all forms of bullying and harassment, including racial harassment, are challenged
- pupils are enabled to participate safely in clothing appropriate to their religious beliefs, particularly in subjects such as science, design and technology and physical education.

Examples for B/3b – securing motivation and concentration

Teachers secure pupils' motivation and concentration by:

- using teaching approaches appropriate to different learning styles
- using, where appropriate, a range of organisational approaches, such as setting, grouping or individual work, to ensure that learning needs are properly addressed
- varying subject content and presentation so that this matches their learning needs
- planning work which builds on their interests and cultural experiences
- planning appropriately challenging work for those whose ability and understanding are in advance of their language skills
- using materials which reflect social and cultural diversity and provide positive images of race, gender and disability
- planning and monitoring the pace of work so that they all have a chance to learn effectively and achieve success
- taking action to maintain interest and continuity of learning for pupils who may be absent for extended periods of time.

Examples for B/3c – providing equality of opportunity

Teaching approaches that provide equality of opportunity include:

- ensuring that boys and girls are able to participate in the same curriculum, particularly in science, design and technology and physical education
- taking account of the interests and concerns of boys and girls by using a range of activities and contexts for work and allowing a variety of interpretations and outcomes, particularly in English, science, design and technology, ICT, art and design, music and physical education
- avoiding gender stereotyping when organising pupils into groups, assigning them to activities or arranging access to equipment, particularly in science, design and technology, ICT, music and physical education
- taking account of pupils' specific religious or cultural beliefs relating to the representation of ideas or experiences or to the use of particular types of equipment, particularly in science, design and technology, ICT and art and design
- enabling the fullest possible participation of pupils with disabilities or particular medical needs in all subjects, offering positive role models and making provision, where necessary, to facilitate access to activities with appropriate support, aids or adaptations. (See **Overcoming potential barriers to learning and assessment for individuals and groups of pupils.**)

ssment approaches
roaches that:
ensure that pupils are given the chance
eir competence and attainment through

ι they have been adequately prepared
imination and stereotyping in any form
ck to pupils to aid further learning.

g

interests and strengths to improve areas
n over time
lp pupils to develop their self-esteem

learning and assessment
pupils

A minority of pupils will have particular learning and assessment
requirements which go beyond the provisions described in sections A and B
and, if not addressed, could create barriers to learning. These requirements
are likely to arise as a consequence of a pupil having a special educational
need or disability or may be linked to a pupil's progress in learning English
as an additional language.

1   Teachers must take account of these requirements and make provision,
    where necessary, to support individuals or groups of pupils to enable them
    to participate effectively in the curriculum and assessment activities. During
    end of key stage assessments, teachers should bear in mind that special
    arrangements are available to support individual pupils.

Pupils with special educational needs

2   Curriculum planning and assessment for pupils with special educational
    needs must take account of the type and extent of the difficulty experienced
    by the pupil. Teachers will encounter a wide range of pupils with special
    educational needs, some of whom will also have disabilities (see paragraphs
    C/4 and C/5). In many cases, the action necessary to respond to an individual's
    requirements for curriculum access will be met through greater differentiation
    of tasks and materials, consistent with school-based intervention as set out
    in the SEN Code of Practice. A smaller number of pupils may need access
    to specialist equipment and approaches or to alternative or adapted activities,
    consistent with school-based intervention augmented by advice and support
    from external specialists as described in the SEN Code of Practice, or, in
    exceptional circumstances, with a statement of special educational need.

Teachers should, where appropriate, work closely with representatives of other agencies who may be supporting the pupil.

3   Teachers should take specific action to provide access to learning for pupils with special educational needs by:
    a   providing for pupils who need help with communication, language and literacy
    b   planning, where necessary, to develop pupils' understanding through the use of all available senses and experiences
    c   planning for pupils' full participation in learning and in physical and practical activities
    d   helping pupils to manage their behaviour, to take part in learning effectively and safely, and, at key stage 4, to prepare for work
    e   helping individuals to manage their emotions, particularly trauma or stress, and to take part in learning.

Examples for C/3a – helping with communication, language and literacy
Teachers provide for pupils who need help with communication, language and literacy through:
- using texts that pupils can read and understand
- using visual and written materials in different formats, including large print, symbol text and Braille
- using ICT, other technological aids and taped materials
- using alternative and augmentative communication, including signs and symbols
- using translators, communicators and amanuenses.

Examples for C/3b – developing understanding
Teachers develop pupils' understanding through the use of all available senses and experiences, by:
- using materials and resources that pupils can access through sight, touch, sound, taste or smell
- using word descriptions and other stimuli to make up for a lack of first-hand experiences
- using ICT, visual and other materials to increase pupils' knowledge of the wider world
- encouraging pupils to take part in everyday activities such as play, drama, class visits and exploring the environment.

Examples for C/3c – planning for full participation
Teachers plan for pupils' full participation in learning and in physical and practical activities through:
- using specialist aids and equipment
- providing support from adults or peers when needed
- adapting tasks or environments
- providing alternative activities, where necessary.

Examples for C/3d – managing behaviour

Teachers help pupils to manage their behaviour, take part in learning
effectively and safely, and, at key stage 4, prepare for work by:

- setting realistic demands and stating them explicitly
- using positive behaviour management, including a clear structure
  of rewards and sanctions
- giving pupils every chance and encouragement to develop the skills
  they need to work well with a partner or a group
- teaching pupils to value and respect the contribution of others
- encouraging and teaching independent working skills
- teaching essential safety rules.

Examples for C/3e – managing emotions

Teachers help individuals manage their emotions and take part
in learning through:

- identifying aspects of learning in which the pupil will engage and
  plan short-term, easily achievable goals in selected activities
- providing positive feedback to reinforce and encourage learning and
  build self-esteem
- selecting tasks and materials sensitively to avoid unnecessary stress
  for the pupil
- creating a supportive learning environment in which the pupil feels
  safe and is able to engage with learning
- allowing time for the pupil to engage with learning and gradually
  increasing the range of activities and demands.

Pupils with disabilities

4   Not all pupils with disabilities will necessarily have special educational needs.
    Many pupils with disabilities learn alongside their peers with little need for
    additional resources beyond the aids which they use as part of their daily life,
    such as a wheelchair, a hearing aid or equipment to aid vision. Teachers must
    take action, however, in their planning to ensure that these pupils are enabled
    to participate as fully and effectively as possible within the National Curriculum
    and the statutory assessment arrangements. Potential areas of difficulty
    should be identified and addressed at the outset of work, without recourse
    to the formal provisions for disapplication.

5   Teachers should take specific action to enable the effective participation
    of pupils with disabilities by:
    a   planning appropriate amounts of time to allow for the satisfactory
        completion of tasks
    b   planning opportunities, where necessary, for the development of skills
        in practical aspects of the curriculum
    c   identifying aspects of programmes of study and attainment targets
        that may present specific difficulties for individuals.

Examples for C/5a – planning to complete tasks

Teachers plan appropriate amounts of time to allow pupils to complete tasks satisfactorily through:

- taking account of the very slow pace at which some pupils will be able to record work, either manually or with specialist equipment, and of the physical effort required
- being aware of the high levels of concentration necessary for some pupils when following or interpreting text or graphics, particularly when using vision aids or tactile methods, and of the tiredness which may result
- allocating sufficient time, opportunity and access to equipment for pupils to gain information through experimental work and detailed observation, including the use of microscopes
- being aware of the effort required by some pupils to follow oral work, whether through use of residual hearing, lip reading or a signer, and of the tiredness or loss of concentration which may occur.

Examples for C/5b – developing skills in practical aspects

Teachers create opportunities for the development of skills in practical aspects of the curriculum through:

- providing adapted, modified or alternative activities or approaches to learning in physical education and ensuring that these have integrity and equivalence to the National Curriculum and enable pupils to make appropriate progress
- providing alternative or adapted activities in science, art and design and design and technology for pupils who are unable to manipulate tools, equipment or materials or who may be allergic to certain types of materials
- ensuring that all pupils can be included and participate safely in geography fieldwork, local studies and visits to museums, historic buildings and sites.

Examples for C/5c – overcoming specific difficulties

Teachers overcome specific difficulties for individuals presented by aspects of the programmes of study and attainment targets through:

- using approaches to enable hearing impaired pupils to learn about sound in science and music
- helping visually impaired pupils to learn about light in science, to access maps and visual resources in geography and to evaluate different products in design and technology and images in art and design
- providing opportunities for pupils to develop strength in depth where they cannot meet the particular requirements of a subject, such as the visual requirements in art and design and the singing requirements in music
- discounting these aspects in appropriate individual cases when required to make a judgement against level descriptions.

Pupils who are learning English as an additional language

6   Pupils for whom English is an additional language have diverse needs in terms of support necessary in English language learning. Planning should take account of such factors as the pupil's age, length of time in this country, previous educational experience and skills in other languages. Careful monitoring of each pupil's progress in the acquisition of English language skills and of subject knowledge and understanding will be necessary to confirm that no learning difficulties are present.

7   The ability of pupils for whom English is an additional language to take part in the National Curriculum may be ahead of their communication skills in English. Teachers should plan learning opportunities to help pupils develop their English and should aim to provide the support pupils need to take part in all subject areas.

8   Teachers should take specific action to help pupils who are learning English as an additional language by:
    a   developing their spoken and written English
    b   ensuring access to the curriculum and to assessment.

Examples for C/8a – developing spoken and written English

Teachers develop pupils' spoken and written English through:

- ensuring that vocabulary work covers both the technical and everyday meaning of key words, metaphors and idioms
- explaining clearly how speaking and writing in English are structured to achieve different purposes, across a range of subjects
- providing a variety of reading material [for example, pupils' own work, the media, ICT, literature, reference books] that highlight the different ways English is used, especially those that help pupils to understand society and culture
- ensuring that there are effective opportunities for talk and that talk is used to support writing in all subjects
- where appropriate, encouraging pupils to transfer their knowledge, skills and understanding of one language to another, pointing out similarities and differences between languages
- building on pupils' experiences of language at home and in the wider community, so that their developing uses of English and other languages support one another.

Examples for C/8b – ensuring access

Teachers make sure pupils have access to the curriculum and to assessment through:

- using accessible texts and materials that suit pupils' ages and levels of learning
- providing support by using ICT or video or audio materials, dictionaries and translators, readers and amanuenses
- using home or first language, where appropriate.

Additional information for mathematics

Teachers may find the following additional information helpful when implementing the statutory inclusion statement: **Providing effective learning opportunities for all pupils.** Teachers need to consider the full requirements of the inclusion statement when planning for individuals or groups of pupils.

To overcome any potential barriers to learning in mathematics, some pupils may require:

- specific help with number recall or the interpretation of data represented in graphs, tables or bar charts, to compensate for difficulties with long- or short-term memory or with visual discrimination
- access to tactile and other specialist equipment for work relating to shape, space and measures, to overcome difficulties in managing visual information
- help in interpreting or responding to oral directions when making mental calculations, to compensate for difficulties in hearing or with auditory discrimination
- access to equipment or other resources, such as ICT to overcome difficulties in thinking and working in the abstract.

In assessment:

- when judgements against level descriptions are required, these should, where appropriate, allow for the provision above.

Use of language across the curriculum

1 Pupils should be taught in all subjects to express themselves correctly and appropriately and to read accurately and with understanding. Since standard English, spoken and written, is the predominant language in which knowledge and skills are taught and learned, pupils should be taught to recognise and use standard English.

Writing

2 In writing, pupils should be taught to use correct spelling and punctuation and follow grammatical conventions. They should also be taught to organise their writing in logical and coherent forms.

Speaking

3 In speaking, pupils should be taught to use language precisely and cogently.

Listening

4 Pupils should be taught to listen to others, and to respond and build on their ideas and views constructively.

Reading

5 In reading, pupils should be taught strategies to help them read with understanding, to locate and use information, to follow a process or argument and summarise, and to synthesise and adapt what they learn from their reading.

6 Pupils should be taught the technical and specialist vocabulary of subjects and how to use and spell these words. They should also be taught to use the patterns of language vital to understanding and expression in different subjects. These include the construction of sentences, paragraphs and texts that are often used in a subject [for example, language to express causality, chronology, logic, exploration, hypothesis, comparison, and how to ask questions and develop arguments].

Use of information and communication technology across the curriculum

1   Pupils should be given opportunities[1] to apply and develop their ICT capability through the use of ICT tools to support their learning in all subjects (with the exception of physical education at key stages 1 and 2).

2   Pupils should be given opportunities to support their work by being taught to:
    a   find things out from a variety of sources, selecting and synthesising the information to meet their needs and developing an ability to question its accuracy, bias and plausibility
    b   develop their ideas using ICT tools to amend and refine their work and enhance its quality and accuracy
    c   exchange and share information, both directly and through electronic media
    d   review, modify and evaluate their work, reflecting critically on its quality, as it progresses.

[1] At key stage 1, there are no statutory requirements to teach the use of ICT in the programmes of study for the non-core foundation subjects. Teachers should use their judgement to decide where it is appropriate to teach the use of ICT across these subjects at key stage 1. At other key stages, there are statutory requirements to use ICT in all subjects, except physical education.

The attainment targets
for mathematics

About the attainment targets

An attainment target sets out the 'knowledge, skills and understanding that pupils of different abilities and maturities are expected to have by the end of each key stage'[1]. Except in the case of citizenship[2], attainment targets consist of eight level descriptions of increasing difficulty, plus a description for exceptional performance above level 8. Each level description describes the types and range of performance that pupils working at that level should characteristically demonstrate.

The level descriptions provide the basis for making judgements about pupils' performance at the end of key stages 1, 2 and 3. At key stage 4, national qualifications are the main means of assessing attainment in mathematics.

Range of levels within which the great majority of pupils are expected to work		Expected attainment for the majority of pupils at the end of the key stage	
Key stage 1	**1–3**	at age 7	**2**
Key stage 2	**2–5**	at age 11	**4**
Key stage 3	**3–7**	at age 14	**5/6**[3]

Assessing attainment at the end of the key stage

In deciding on a pupil's level of attainment at the end of a key stage, teachers should judge which description best fits the pupil's performance. When doing so each description should be considered alongside descriptions for adjacent levels.

Arrangements for statutory assessment at the end of each key stage are set out in detail in QCA's annual booklets about assessment and reporting arrangements.

Examples in the level descriptions

The examples in grey type are not statutory.

[1] As defined by The Education Act 1996, section 353a.
[2] In citizenship, expected performance for the majority of pupils at the end of key stages 3 and 4 is set out in end of key stage descriptions.
[3] Including modern foreign languages.

Level 5

In order to carry through tasks and solve mathematical problems, pupils identify and obtain necessary information. They check their results, considering whether these are sensible. Pupils show understanding of situations by describing them mathematically using symbols, words and diagrams. They draw simple conclusions of their own and give an explanation of their reasoning.

Level 6

Pupils carry through substantial tasks and solve quite complex problems by independently breaking them down into smaller, more manageable tasks. They interpret, discuss and synthesise information presented in a variety of mathematical forms. Pupils' writing explains and informs their use of diagrams. Pupils are beginning to give mathematical justifications.

Level 7

Starting from problems or contexts that have been presented to them, pupils progressively refine or extend the mathematics used to generate fuller solutions. They give a reason for their choice of mathematical presentation, explaining features they have selected. Pupils justify their generalisations, arguments or solutions, showing some insight into the mathematical structure of the problem. They appreciate the difference between mathematical explanation and experimental evidence.

Level 8

Pupils develop and follow alternative approaches. They reflect on their own lines of enquiry when exploring mathematical tasks; in doing so they introduce and use a range of mathematical techniques. Pupils convey mathematical or statistical meaning through precise and consistent use of symbols that is sustained throughout the work. They examine generalisations or solutions reached in an activity, commenting constructively on the reasoning and logic or the process employed, or the results obtained, and make further progress in the activity as a result.

Exceptional performance

Pupils give reasons for the choices they make when investigating within mathematics itself or when using mathematics to analyse tasks; these reasons explain why particular lines of enquiry or procedures are followed and others rejected. Pupils apply the mathematics they know in familiar and unfamiliar contexts. Pupils use mathematical language and symbols effectively in presenting a convincing reasoned argument. Their reports include mathematical justifications, explaining their solutions to problems involving a number of features or variables.

Attainment target 1: using and applying mathematics

Teachers should expect attainment at a given level in this attainment target to be demonstrated through activities in which the mathematics from the other attainment targets is at, or very close to, the same level.

Level 1

Pupils use mathematics as an integral part of classroom activities. They represent their work with objects or pictures and discuss it. They recognise and use a simple pattern or relationship.

Level 2

Pupils select the mathematics they use in some classroom activities. They discuss their work using mathematical language and are beginning to represent it using symbols and simple diagrams. They explain why an answer is correct.

Level 3

Pupils try different approaches and find ways of overcoming difficulties that arise when they are solving problems. They are beginning to organise their work and check results. Pupils discuss their mathematical work and are beginning to explain their thinking. They use and interpret mathematical symbols and diagrams. Pupils show that they understand a general statement by finding particular examples that match it.

Level 4

Pupils are developing their own strategies for solving problems and are using these strategies both in working within mathematics and in applying mathematics to practical contexts. They present information and results in a clear and organised way. They search for a solution by trying out ideas of their own.

Level 5

Pupils use their understanding of place value to multiply and divide whole numbers and decimals by 10, 100 and 1000. They order, add and subtract negative numbers in context. They use all four operations with decimals to two places. They reduce a fraction to its simplest form by cancelling common factors and solve simple problems involving ratio and direct proportion. They calculate fractional or percentage parts of quantities and measurements, using a calculator where appropriate. Pupils understand and use an appropriate non-calculator method for solving problems that involve multiplying and dividing any three-digit number by any two-digit number. They check their solutions by applying inverse operations or estimating using approximations. They construct, express in symbolic form, and use simple formulae involving one or two operations. They use brackets appropriately. Pupils use and interpret coordinates in all four quadrants.

Level 6

Pupils order and approximate decimals when solving numerical problems and equations [for example, $x^3 + x = 20$], using trial-and-improvement methods. Pupils are aware of which number to consider as 100 per cent, or a whole, in problems involving comparisons, and use this to evaluate one number as a fraction or percentage of another. They understand and use the equivalences between fractions, decimals and percentages, and calculate using ratios in appropriate situations. They add and subtract fractions by writing them with a common denominator. When exploring number sequences, pupils find and describe in words the rule for the next term or nth term of a sequence where the rule is linear. They formulate and solve linear equations with whole-number coefficients. They represent mappings expressed algebraically, and use Cartesian coordinates for graphical representation interpreting general features.

Level 7

In making estimates, pupils round to one significant figure and multiply and divide mentally. They understand the effects of multiplying and dividing by numbers between 0 and 1. Pupils solve numerical problems involving multiplication and division with numbers of any size, using a calculator efficiently and appropriately. They understand and use proportional changes, calculating the result of any proportional change using only multiplicative methods. Pupils find and describe in symbols the next term or nth term of a sequence where the rule is quadratic; they multiply two expressions of the form $(x + n)$; they simplify the corresponding quadratic expressions. Pupils use algebraic and graphical methods to solve simultaneous linear equations in two variables. They solve simple inequalities.

Level 8

Pupils solve problems involving calculating with powers, roots and numbers expressed in standard form, checking for correct order of magnitude. They choose to use fractions or percentages to solve problems involving repeated proportional changes or the calculation of the original quantity given the result of a proportional change. They evaluate algebraic formulae, substituting fractions, decimals and negative numbers. They calculate one variable, given the others, in formulae such as $V = \pi r^2 h$. Pupils manipulate algebraic formulae, equations and expressions, finding common factors and multiplying two linear expressions. They know that $a^2 - b^2 = (a+b)(a-b)$. They solve inequalities in two variables. Pupils sketch and interpret graphs of linear, quadratic, cubic and reciprocal functions, and graphs that model real situations.

Exceptional performance

Pupils understand and use rational and irrational numbers. They determine the bounds of intervals. Pupils understand and use direct and inverse proportion. In simplifying algebraic expressions, they use rules of indices for negative and fractional values. In finding formulae that approximately connect data, pupils express general laws in symbolic form. They solve simultaneous equations in two variables where one equation is linear and the other is quadratic. They solve problems using intersections and gradients of graphs.

Attainment target 2: number and algebra

Level 1

Pupils count, order, add and subtract numbers when solving problems involving up to 10 objects. They read and write the numbers involved.

Level 2

Pupils count sets of objects reliably, and use mental recall of addition and subtraction facts to 10. They begin to understand the place value of each digit in a number and use this to order numbers up to 100. They choose the appropriate operation when solving addition and subtraction problems. They use the knowledge that subtraction is the inverse of addition. They use mental calculation strategies to solve number problems involving money and measures. They recognise sequences of numbers, including odd and even numbers.

Level 3

Pupils show understanding of place value in numbers up to 1000 and use this to make approximations. They begin to use decimal notation and to recognise negative numbers, in contexts such as money and temperature. Pupils use mental recall of addition and subtraction facts to 20 in solving problems involving larger numbers. They add and subtract numbers with two digits mentally and numbers with three digits using written methods. They use mental recall of the 2, 3, 4, 5 and 10 multiplication tables and derive the associated division facts. They solve whole-number problems involving multiplication or division, including those that give rise to remainders. They use simple fractions that are several parts of a whole and recognise when two simple fractions are equivalent.

Level 4

Pupils use their understanding of place value to multiply and divide whole numbers by 10 or 100. In solving number problems, pupils use a range of mental methods of computation with the four operations, including mental recall of multiplication facts up to 10×10 and quick derivation of corresponding division facts. They use efficient written methods of addition and subtraction and of short multiplication and division. They add and subtract decimals to two places and order decimals to three places. In solving problems with or without a calculator, pupils check the reasonableness of their results by reference to their knowledge of the context or to the size of the numbers. They recognise approximate proportions of a whole and use simple fractions and percentages to describe these. Pupils recognise and describe number patterns, and relationships including multiple, factor and square. They begin to use simple formulae expressed in words. Pupils use and interpret coordinates in the first quadrant.

Acknowledgements

About the work used in this document
The artwork and photographs used in this book are the result of a national selection organised by QCA and the Design Council. We would like to thank all 3,108 pupils who took part and especially the following pupils and schools whose work has been used throughout the National Curriculum.

Pupils Frankie Allen, Sarah Anderson, Naomi Ball, Kristina Battleday, Ashley Boyle, Martin Broom, Katie Brown, Alex Bryant, Tania Burnett, Elizabeth Burrows, Caitie Calloway, Kavandeep Chahal, Donna Clarke, Leah Cliffe, Megan Coombs, Andrew Cornford, Samantha Davidoff, Jodie Evans, Holly Fowler, Rachel Fort, Christopher Fort, Hannah Foster, Ruth Fry, Nicholas Furlonge, Tasleem Ghanchi, Rebecca Goodwin, Megan Goodwin, Joanna Gray, Alisha Grazette, Emma Habbeshon, Zoe Hall, Kay Hampshire, Jessica Harris, Aimee Howard, Amy Hurst, Katherine Hymers, Safwan Ismael, Tamaszina Jacobs-Abiola, Tomi Johnson, Richard Jones, Bruno Jones, Thomas Kelleher, Sophie Lambert, Gareth Lloyd, Ope Majekodunmi, Sophie Manchester, Alex Massie, Amy McNair, Dale Meachen, Katherine Mills, Rebecca Moore, Andrew Morgan, Amber Murrell, Sally O'Connor, Rosie O'Reilly, Antonia Pain, Daniel Pamment, Jennie Plant, Christopher Prest, Megan Ramsay, Alice Ross, David Rowles, Amy Sandford, Zeba Saudagar, Nathan Scarfe, Daniel Scully, Bilal Shakoor, Sandeep Sharma, Morrad Siyahla, Daryl Smith, Catriona Statham, Scott Taylor, Amy Thornton, Jessica Tidmarsh, Alix Tinkler, Lucy Titford, Marion Tulloch, Charlotte Ward, Kaltuun Warsame, Emily Webb, Bradley West, Daniel Wilkinson, Soriah Williams, Susan Williamson, Helen Williamson, Charlotte Windmill, Ryan Wollan, Olivia Wright.

Schools Adam's Grammar School, Almondbury Junior School, Bishops Castle Community College, Bolton Brow Junior and Infant School, Boxford C of E Voluntary Controlled Primary School, Bugbrooke School, Cantell School, Charnwood Primary School, Cheselbourne County First School, Chester Catholic High School, Dales Infant School, Deanery C of E High School, Driffield C of E Infants' School, Dursley Primary School, Fourfields County Primary School, Furze Infants School, Gosforth High School, Grahame Park Junior School, Green Park Combined School, Gusford Community Primary School, Hartshill School, Headington School, Holyport Manor School, Jersey College for Girls Preparatory School, King Edward VI School, King James's School, Kingsway Junior School, Knutsford High School, Leiston Primary School, Maltby Manor Infant School, Mullion Comprehensive School, North Marston C of E First School, Norton Hill School, Penglais School, Priory Secondary School, Redknock School, Richard Whittington Primary School, Ringwood School, Sarah Bonnell School, Sedgemoor Manor Infants School, Selly Park Technology College for Girls, Southwark Infant School, St Albans High School for Girls, St Denys C of E Infant School, St Helen's C of E (Aided) Primary School, St John's Infants School, St Joseph's RC Infant School, St Laurence School, St Mary Magdalene School, St Matthews C of E Aided Primary School, St Michael's C of E School, St Saviour's and St Olave's School, St Thomas The Martyr C of E Primary School, Sawtry Community College, The Duchess's High School, Tideway School, Torfield School, Trinity C of E Primary School, Upper Poppelton School, Walton High School.

QCA and the Design Council would also like to thank the figures from public life who contributed their ideas about the value of each curriculum subject.

Attainment target 4: handling data

The attainment target does not apply at key stage 1.

Level 1
Pupils sort objects and classify them, demonstrating the criterion they have used.

Level 2
Pupils sort objects and classify them using more than one criterion. When they have gathered information, pupils record results in simple lists, tables and block graphs, in order to communicate their findings.

Level 3
Pupils extract and interpret information presented in simple tables and lists. They construct bar charts and pictograms, where the symbol represents a group of units, to communicate information they have gathered, and they interpret information presented to them in these forms.

Level 4
Pupils collect discrete data and record them using a frequency table. They understand and use the mode and range to describe sets of data. They group data, where appropriate, in equal class intervals, represent collected data in frequency diagrams and interpret such diagrams. They construct and interpret simple line graphs.

Level 5

Pupils understand and use the mean of discrete data. They compare two simple distributions, using the range and one of the mode, median or mean. They interpret graphs and diagrams, including pie charts, and draw conclusions. They understand and use the probability scale from 0 to 1. Pupils find and justify probabilities, and approximations to these, by selecting and using methods based on equally likely outcomes and experimental evidence, as appropriate. They understand that different outcomes may result from repeating an experiment.

Level 6

Pupils collect and record continuous data, choosing appropriate equal class intervals over a sensible range to create frequency tables. They construct and interpret frequency diagrams. They construct pie charts. Pupils draw conclusions from scatter diagrams, and have a basic understanding of correlation. When dealing with a combination of two experiments, pupils identify all the outcomes, using diagrammatic, tabular or other forms of communication. In solving problems, they use their knowledge that the total probability of all the mutually exclusive outcomes of an experiment is 1.

Level 7

Pupils specify hypotheses and test them by designing and using appropriate methods that take account of variability or bias. They determine the modal class and estimate the mean, median and range of sets of grouped data, selecting the statistic most appropriate to their line of enquiry. They use measures of average and range, with associated frequency polygons, as appropriate, to compare distributions and make inferences. They draw a line of best fit on a scatter diagram, by inspection. Pupils understand relative frequency as an estimate of probability and use this to compare outcomes of experiments.

Level 8

Pupils interpret and construct cumulative frequency tables and diagrams, using the upper boundary of the class interval. They estimate the median and interquartile range and use these to compare distributions and make inferences. They understand how to calculate the probability of a compound event and use this in solving problems.

Exceptional performance

Pupils interpret and construct histograms. They understand how different methods of sampling and different sample sizes may affect the reliability of conclusions drawn. They select and justify a sample and method to investigate a population. They recognise when and how to work with probabilities associated with independent mutually exclusive events.

Attainment target 3: shape, space and measures

Level 1

When working with 2-D and 3-D shapes, pupils use everyday language to describe properties and positions. They measure and order objects using direct comparison, and order events.

Level 2

Pupils use mathematical names for common 3-D and 2-D shapes and describe their properties, including numbers of sides and corners. They distinguish between straight and turning movements, understand angle as a measurement of turn, and recognise right angles in turns. They begin to use everyday non-standard and standard units to measure length and mass.

Level 3

Pupils classify 3-D and 2-D shapes in various ways using mathematical properties such as reflective symmetry for 2-D shapes. They use non-standard units, standard metric units of length, capacity and mass, and standard units of time, in a range of contexts.

Level 4

Pupils make 3-D mathematical models by linking given faces or edges, draw common 2-D shapes in different orientations on grids. They reflect simple shapes in a mirror line. They choose and use appropriate units and instruments, interpreting, with appropriate accuracy, numbers on a range of measuring instruments. They find perimeters of simple shapes and find areas by counting squares.

Level 5

When constructing models and when drawing or using shapes, pupils measure and draw angles to the nearest degree, and use language associated with angle. Pupils know the angle sum of a triangle and that of angles at a point. They identify all the symmetries of 2-D shapes. They know the rough metric equivalents of imperial units still in daily use and convert one metric unit to another. They make sensible estimates of a range of measures in relation to everyday situations. Pupils understand and use the formula for the area of a rectangle.

Level 6

Pupils recognise and use common 2-D representations of 3-D objects. They know and use the properties of quadrilaterals in classifying different types of quadrilateral. They solve problems using angle and symmetry properties of polygons and angle properties of intersecting and parallel lines, and explain these properties. They devise instructions for a computer to generate and transform shapes and paths. They understand and use appropriate formulae for finding circumferences and areas of circles, areas of plane rectilinear figures and volumes of cuboids when solving problems. They enlarge shapes by a positive whole-number scale factor.

Level 7

Pupils understand and apply Pythagoras' theorem when solving problems in two dimensions. They calculate lengths, areas and volumes in plane shapes and right prisms. Pupils enlarge shapes by a fractional scale factor, and appreciate the similarity of the resulting shapes. They determine the locus of an object moving according to a rule. Pupils appreciate the imprecision of measurement and recognise that a measurement given to the nearest whole number may be inaccurate by up to one half in either direction. They understand and use compound measures, such as speed.

Level 8

Pupils understand and use congruence and mathematical similarity. They use sine, cosine and tangent in right-angled triangles when solving problems in two dimensions. They distinguish between formulae for perimeter, area and volume, by considering dimensions.

Exceptional performance

Pupils sketch the graphs of sine, cosine and tangent functions for any angle, and generate and interpret graphs based on these functions. Pupils use sine, cosine and tangent of angles of any size, and Pythagoras' theorem when solving problems in two and three dimensions. They use the conditions for congruent triangles in formal geometric proofs [for example, to prove that the base angles of an isosceles triangle are equal]. They calculate lengths of circular arcs and areas of sectors, and calculate the surface area of cylinders and volumes of cones and spheres. Pupils appreciate the continuous nature of scales that are used to make measurements.